The
FOCALGUIDE
to
Home Proce

THE (f) FOCALGUIDES TO

Basic Photography	BETTER PICTURES	David Lynch
	COLOUR	David Lynch
	EFFECTS AND TRICKS	Günter Spitzing
	EXPOSURE	David Lynch
	LIGHTING	Paul Petzold
	LOW LIGHT PHOTOGRAPHY	Paul Petzold
	SELLING YOUR PHOTOGRAPHS	Ed Buziak
	SLIDES	Graham Saxby
Equipment	CAMERA ACCESSORIES	Leonard Gaunt
	CAMERAS	Clyde Reynolds
	FILTERS	Clyde Reynolds
	FLASH	Günter Spitzing
	LARGER FORMAT CAMERAS	Sidney Ray
	LENSES	Leonard Gaunt
	SLIDE-TAPE	Brian Duncalf
	35 mm	Leonard Gaunt
	THE 35 mm SINGLE LENS REFLEX	Leonard Gaunt
Processing	CIBACHROME	Jack H. Coote
	COLOUR FILM PROCESSING	Derek Watkins
	COLOUR PRINTING	Jack H. Coote
	ENLARGING	Günter Spitzing
	HOME PROCESSING	Ralph Jacobson
	THE DARKROOM	Leonard Gaunt
Subjects	ACTION PHOTOGRAPHY	Don Morley
	BIRD PHOTOGRAPHY	Michael W. Richards
	CLOSE-UPS	Sidney Ray
	MOUNTAINS	Douglas Milner
	PHOTOGRAPHING PEOPLE	Alison Trapmore
	PHOTOGRAPHING PLACES	D. H. Day
	PLANTS AND FLOWERS	David Walton
	PORTRAITS	Günter Spitzing
	WEDDINGS AND SPECIAL OCCASIONS	Bob Bluffield
	TRAVEL PHOTOGRAPHY	Peter McKenzie
Movie	MOVIE TITLING	Philip Jenkins
	MOVIEMAKING	Paul Petzold
	SHOOTING ANIMATION	Zoran Perisic

The FOCALGUIDE to Home Processing

Colour and Monochrome Materials

R E Jacobson

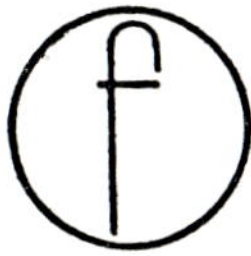

Focal Press

London & Boston

Focal Press
is an imprint of the Butterworth Group
which has principal offices in
London, Boston, Durban, Singapore, Sydney, Toronto, Wellington

First published 1973
Reprinted 1974, 1975, 1976 (twice), 1977
Second edition 1978
Reprinted 1980, 1982

In Spanish: *El Revelado Amateur*, Ediciones Omega SA, Barcelona
In Portuguese: *Guia Prático da Revelação*, Editorial Presença Lda, Lisbon

British Library Cataloguing in Publication Data

Jacobson, Ralph Eric
The Focalguide to home processing — 2nd ed.
1. Photography — Processing
I. Title
770'.28 TR287

ISBN 0 240 51017 8

Printed and bound in Great Britain by
Maund & Irvine Ltd., Tring, Herts.

Contents

PROCESSING COLOUR NEGATIVE FILMS

REVERSAL PROCESSING OF BLACK-AND-WHITE FILMS

Types of Processing

If you are the sort of person who likes finding out how things work, processing your own films is an ideal way to obtain a better understanding of the photographic process. There is, of course, the personal satisfaction in having achieved your own results – often very shortly after having taken the photographs, whereas sending your films away for processing may take anything from 24 hours to a few weeks before seeing the results.

The time spent on doing your own processing is not long; it may take less than half an hour for the rapid processing of black-and-white negative films to approximately one hour for processing colour reversal films, once the processing solutions have been made up. When you are sufficiently experienced, it is a routine process that need not claim your undivided attention. You can catch up with your correspondence, read a book, listen to music, etc, at the same time.

The most important advantage in doing your own processing is that mastery of a few simple techniques allows you to exercise complete control over the required results. Moreover, you can give your films the individual and personal treatment that they deserve and carry out special processes which few processing laboratories undertake. Making black-and-white slides, for example, is easy and inexpensive if you do it yourself, but a commercial service is not readily available.

Another important advantage of home-processing is cost. You can buy chemicals for processing your colour reversal films at approximately half the cost of sending them away to be processed, and processing black-and-white negative films works out at considerably less than half the price of commercial processing. So, even taking into account the small initial outlay in buying the necessary equipment, doing your own processing should pay for itself within a relatively short period.

The equipment required for processing is simple and cheap and it is possible to do without a darkroom. If you can take photographs, there is no reason why you should not be able to process your own films, because the procedure is only slightly more complicated than pressing the shutter release, and requires only a few manipulative skills that can be quickly acquired by almost anyone.

Elements of processing

Having said how advantageous it is to do your own processing, I shall now define exactly what the word means.

Processing is the continuation to completion of the effect of light on the film which you start by pressing the shutter release of the camera. When you press the button, the film records the scene that is being photographed. However, the image on the film is neither visible nor permanent and has been given the name latent image. The means by which this latent image is made visible and permanent is known as processing.

The general procedure involved in processing films consists of immersing the film in various solutions for specified times, followed by a wash to remove all unwanted chemicals and a final drying to yield a permanent record of the original scene.

This simple sequence represents a general procedure for obtaining a permanent record and applies to all types of processing, whether the objective is a negative or positive in either black-and-white or colour. The complexity of processing does, however, vary with the type of process: processing of black-and-white negative films is the simplest, whereas processing of colour reversal films (also called positives or transparencies) is the most complex with respect to the number of processing solutions and operations involved. But all processing operations are simple and easy to carry out, whatever the film being processed.

In order to understand a little bit more about processing, let us consider the processing of a black-and-white negative film in greater detail. Two processing solutions are used in succession, the first is the developer and the second is the fixer. The developer has the function of amplifying (or making visible) the original invisible latent image. The developer acts by converting the silver halides present in the film coating (emulsion) to black metallic silver *only* in those areas that were exposed to light.

The main function of the fixer is to remove the light-sensitive constituents (silver halides) of the film from those areas that had not received sufficient light to form a latent image. To complete the processing sequence, washing

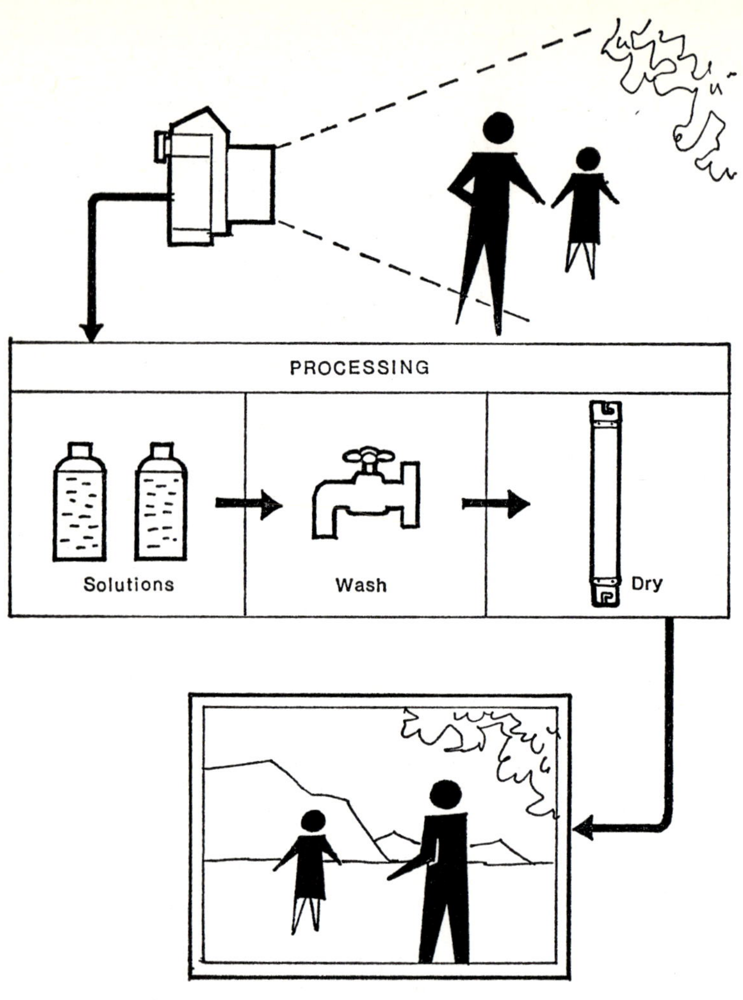

After exposure in the camera, the film is passed through the processing solutions, washed and dried. The final result is a print or transparency providing a permanent image of the original scene

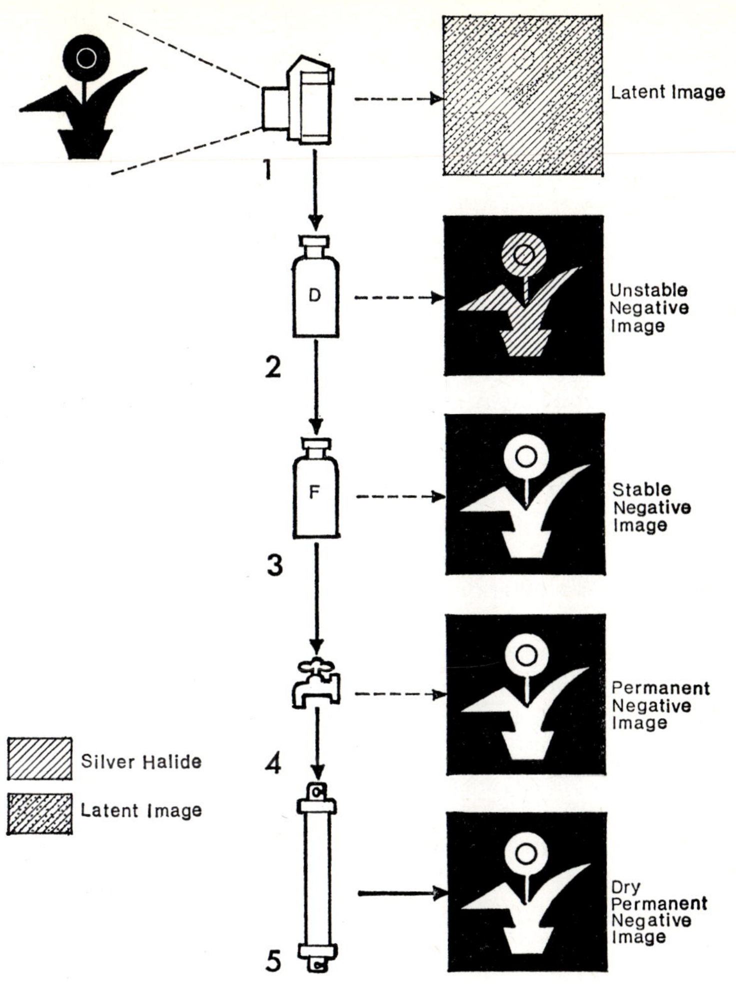

Formation of a negative. 1, Exposure forms a latent image (actually invisible). 2, Development amplifies the image and makes it visible but unstable. 3, After an intermediate rinse, fixing removes the unexposed silver halide and provides a stable image. 4, Washing removes the residual chemicals. 5, When dry, the image is stable and permanent.

followed by drying removes all unwanted chemicals from the film to give a dry permanent negative image of the original scene.

From negative to positive

From a comparison of the subject with the final negative image you can see that the tones are reversed, i.e. the black plant on a white background appears on the negative as a white plant on a black background (page 13).

This, however, is an unrealistic subject as just about all the scenes that you will photograph will consist not only of black and white areas, but also of intermediate tones or shades of grey.

In black-and-white photography, intermediate tones or shades of grey are formed from all objects whatever their colour, and these tones are related to the brightness of the original colours.

If we now consider a more realistic scene such as photographing a white house, what does the negative look like? The brightest areas of the scene – namely, the white house and cloud – appear almost black in the negative, while the dark areas, such as the shadow areas in the doors and windows, are almost transparent. The intermediate tones of the bright sky, the less bright green grass, the dark red roof and grey path are reproduced in the negative as shades of grey, gradually increasing in lightness. (page 15)

Thus, in a negative the tones of the original scene are recorded in the opposite sense, and to complete the cycle a positive print is made by exposing a light sensitive paper, similar to the film in the camera, using the negative as the original and shining light through it. This procedure is known as printing and can be carried out by placing the negative in direct contact with the paper and exposing the negative/paper sandwich to a light source. This results in a print the same size as the negative and has been given the name contact printing. Alternatively, an *enlarger* may be used, in which case a print of almost any size can be made. (Page 16).

These are separate operations from processing films, but are just as easy to carry out. In fact, after exposing the paper in a

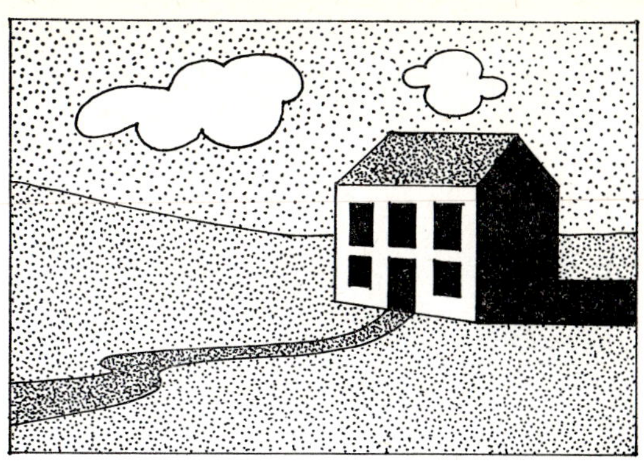

ORIGINAL SCENE

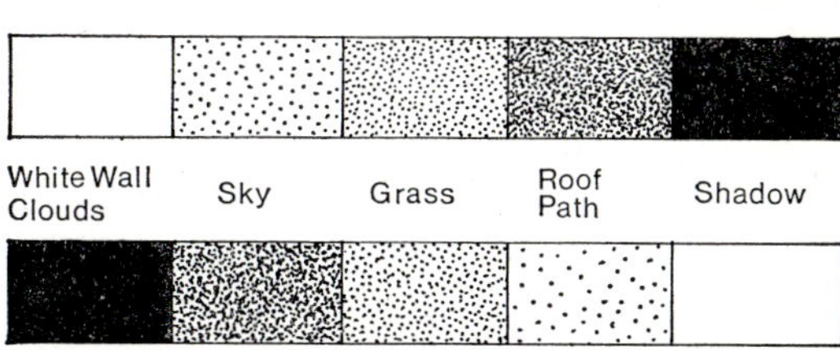

NEGATIVE

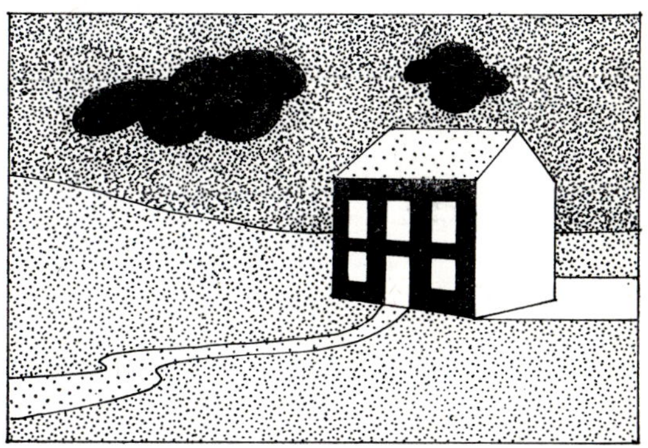

A negative is a tonally reversed image of the original scene. The effect of light amplified by development blackens the emulsion so that the lighter the tones of the original the greater the density in the negative.

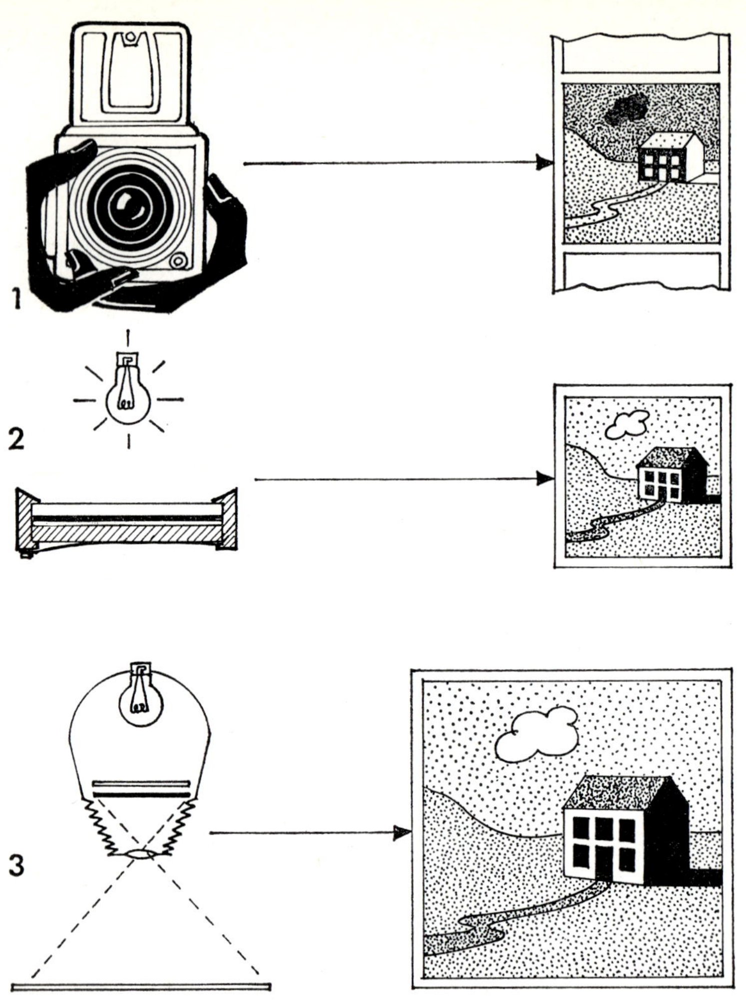

From negative to print. 1, Exposure plus processing provide the negative. 2, Contact printing provides a print the same size as the negative. 3, Projection printing provides prints of increased or reduced size.

contact printer or enlarger, the processing sequences which follow are almost identical to those used for processing the negative film.

Reversal processing of black and white films

Up until now, only negative processes have been considered, in which the brightest parts of the scene are reproduced as the blackest areas on the negative. You saw that the processing of negatives is relatively simple and a positive reproduction of the original scene can be made by printing from the negative. If the negative is printed on film material, a positive transparency results. However, it is possible to obtain a positive transparency directly, without first forming a negative and then printing – this is known as reversal processing.

Reversal processing is especially useful for ciné films and for colour films (see page 25). The purpose of reversal processing is the exact opposite of that involved in negative processing and results in the formation of a positive from a positive. It provides a *single* copy which is generally viewed via a projector. Duplicate negatives can also be made if required by printing the negative on to a film which is then reversal processed.

The processing sequences involved in reversal processing are more numerous than those of negative processing. The exposed film is first developed in a developer, which ensures that the latent image is fully developed: this is known as the first or primary development. The negative silver image so formed is next completely dissolved away by a bleach. The originally unexposed areas of the film are then fully exposed: this forms a latent image which can then be developed in the secondary developer to form a positive image. The processing steps which follow are the same as those used for negative processing, i.e. fixing, washing and drying.

Any sensitive material can be reversal processed, but those intended for it are generally specially manufactured. Fortunately, however, processing kits are commercially available for the reversal processing of most currently available black-and-white negative films.

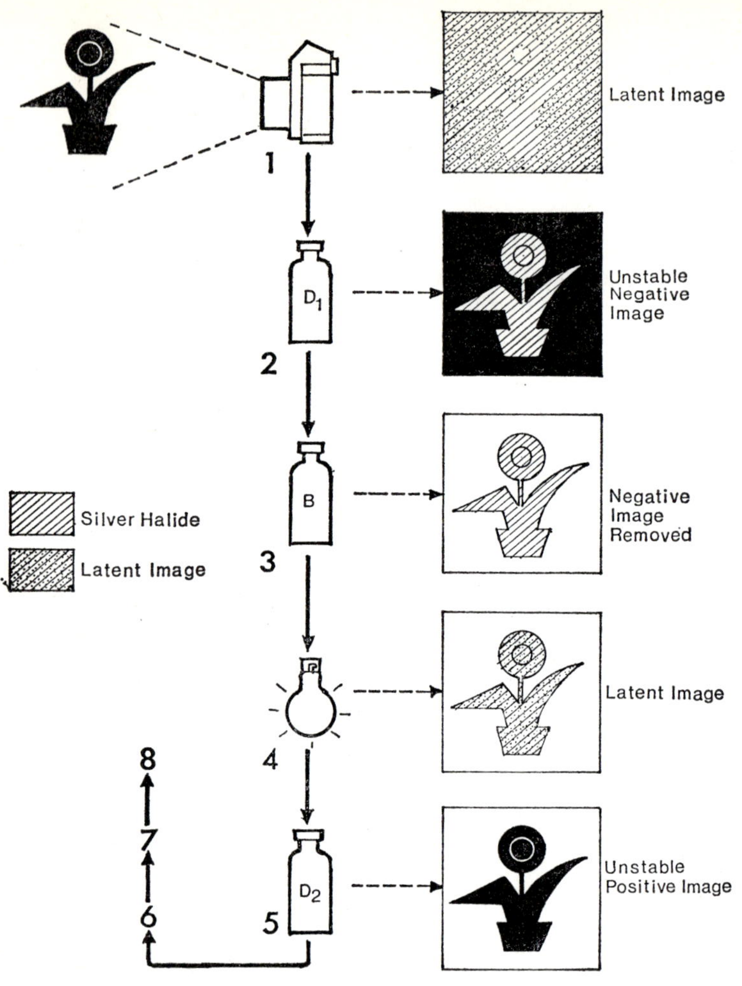

Reversal processing. 1, Exposure produces a latent negative image. 2, First development provides an unstable negative image. 3, Bleaching removes the negative image. 4, Re-exposure produces a latent positive image. 5, Second development provides an unstable positive image. 6,7,8, Fixing, washing and drying make the positive image stable and permanent. Intermediate rinses have been omitted from this summary of procedure.

Structure of the colour negative

A colour negative has a somewhat strange appearance because it is not only opposite in tone, but also opposite in colour to the original scene. Suppose that you take a photograph of a red flower with green leaves in a blue flower pot, what does the negative look like? The processed film gives an image in which all the tones and colours are reversed: blacks become white and whites become black, just as we saw earlier for black-and-white negatives. The colours are also reproduced as opposites or complementaries – the red flower appears cyan, the green leaves appear magenta, and the blue pot appears yellow, where cyan, magenta and yellow are termed complementary colours or subtractive primary colours (see page 22). The appearance of most modern colour negative materials is further complicated by an overall orange-yellow colour which also extends into the border areas. This colouration is quite normal and is known as a mask, which leads to more accurate colour reproduction at the printing stage.

To the uninitiated, the appearance of colour negatives and the reasons for reproducing colours as opposites might seem obscure. In order to understand the reproduction of colour by a colour negative process, it helps if we consider the principles on which it is based.

What is commonly known as 'white light' consists of all the visible colours of the spectrum: red, orange, yellow, green, blue, indigo and violet. For the purposes of colour reproduction, these seven spectral colours are divided into three regions: red, green and blue, which are known as the additive primary colours. The reason for doing this is that experiments have shown that any colour can be formed by mixing together the appropriate amounts of red, green and blue light. In colour reproduction, any colour can be reproduced by separately recording the amounts of red, green and blue light reflected by the subject and recombining them at a later stage.

Colour negative films contain what amount to three negatives in one: one to record the red light, the second to record the green light, and the third to record the blue light reflected by the coloured object being photographed. *Integral tripacks* form

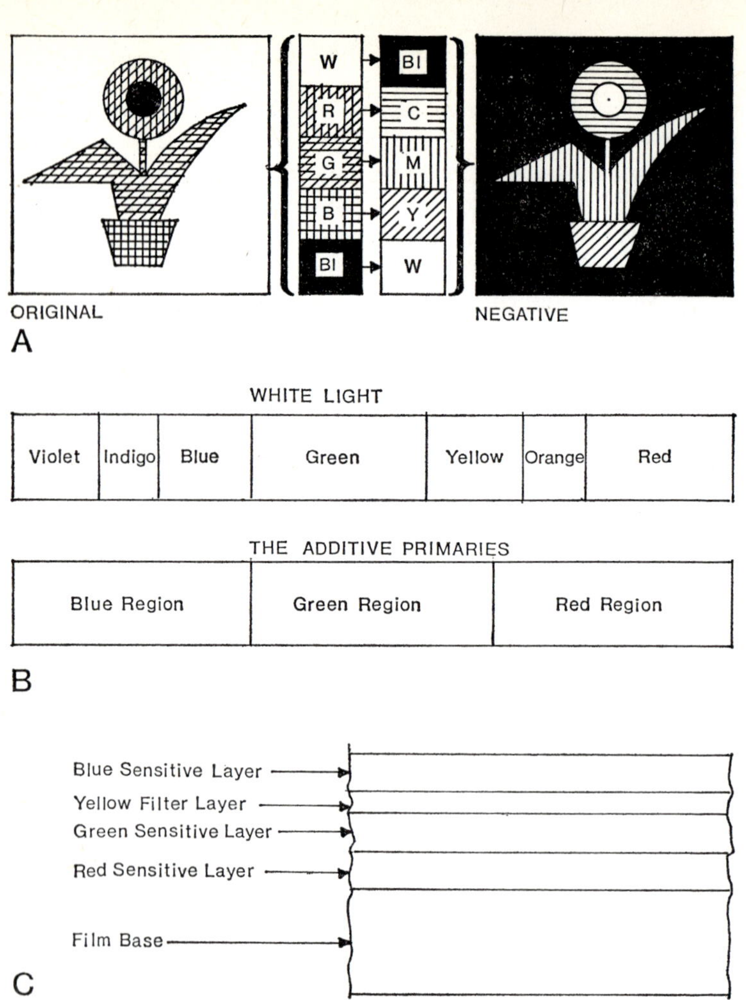

Colour negative. **A**, Colour negatives are opposite in both tone and hue to the original scene. **B**, The components of white light can be grouped as red, green and blue. These are the additive primaries. **C**, Integral tripacks, with three light sensitive layers, form the basis of all modern colour materials.

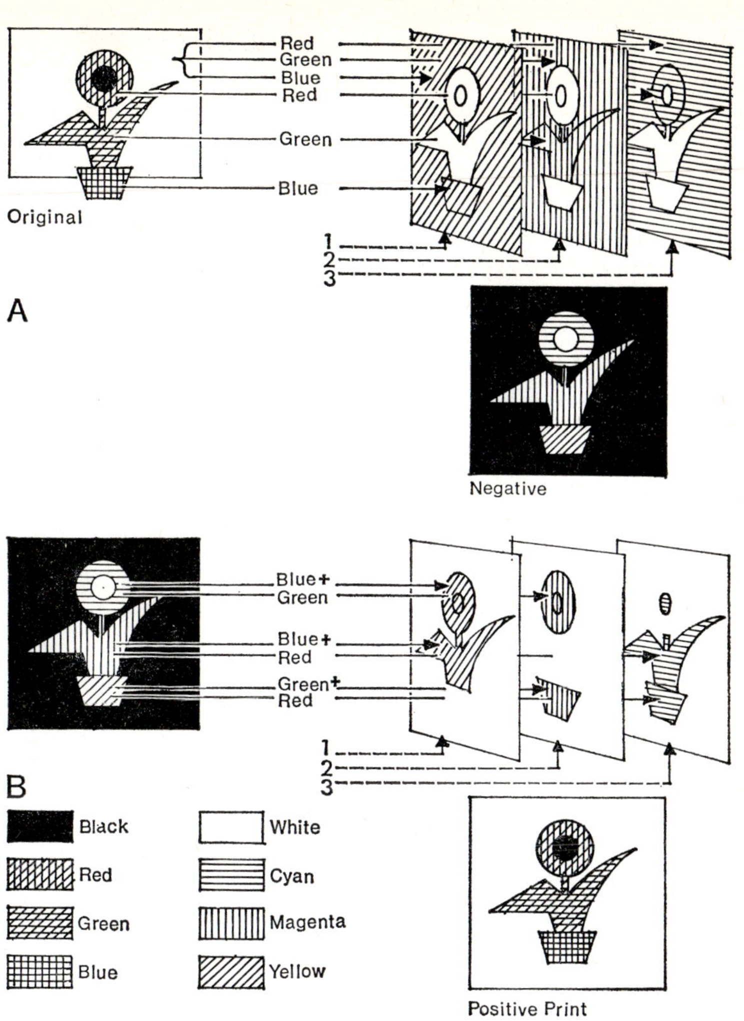

Negative positive colour. **A**, Colours from the original affect different layers of the film. 1, Blue-sensitive layer. 2, Green-sensitive ayer. 3, Red-sensitive layer. **B**, When tripack colour paper is exposed through the negative, a similar process provides a print in natural colour.

the basis of modern colour films, in which a red sensitive layer is coated on the film base, followed by a green sensitive layer, a yellow filter layer and a blue sensitive layer (see page 20). The yellow filter layer is used to absorb blue light to which the green and red sensitive layers are also slightly sensitive.

After exposing and processing a colour negative film, the blue sensitive layer records the blue light and forms a yellow image, the green sensitive layer records the green light and forms a magenta image, and the red sensitive layer records the red light and forms a cyan image. These image colours are governed, of course, by the dyes incorporated in the emulsion. They could be any colour, but these complementaries are the most suitable for recreating the original colours in the final print. To explain why, let us first consider how complementary colours are defined: you saw earlier that white light consists of the three additive primary colours – red, green and blue. If we subtract each of the three additive primary colours in turn from white, we obtain the three *subtractive primary colours (or complementary colours):*

White = Red + Green + Blue
White minus Red = Green + Blue (appears Cyan)
White minus Green = Red + Blue (appears Magenta)
White minus Blue = Red + Green (appears Yellow)

Thus, the complementary colour to red is *minus red* or *cyan,* the complementary colour to green is *minus green* or *magenta,* and the complementary colour to blue is *minus blue* or *yellow.*

Colour negatives are printed by a similar method to that used for enlarging black-and-white negatives. In this case, an integral tripack paper is used, which is similar in its construction to the colour negative film – i.e. it also contains separate blue, green and red sensitive layers.

A red area of the original forms a cyan image in the red sensitive layer of the negative. When the paper is exposed, this cyan image affects the green and blue sensitive layers, but not the red layer because the cyan 'filter' removes red from the white exposing light. Again, the dyes used are cyan, magenta and yellow, but this time magenta dye is produced in the green sensitive layer and yellow in the blue sensitive layer. When these dyes are seen superimposed, they remove green and blue

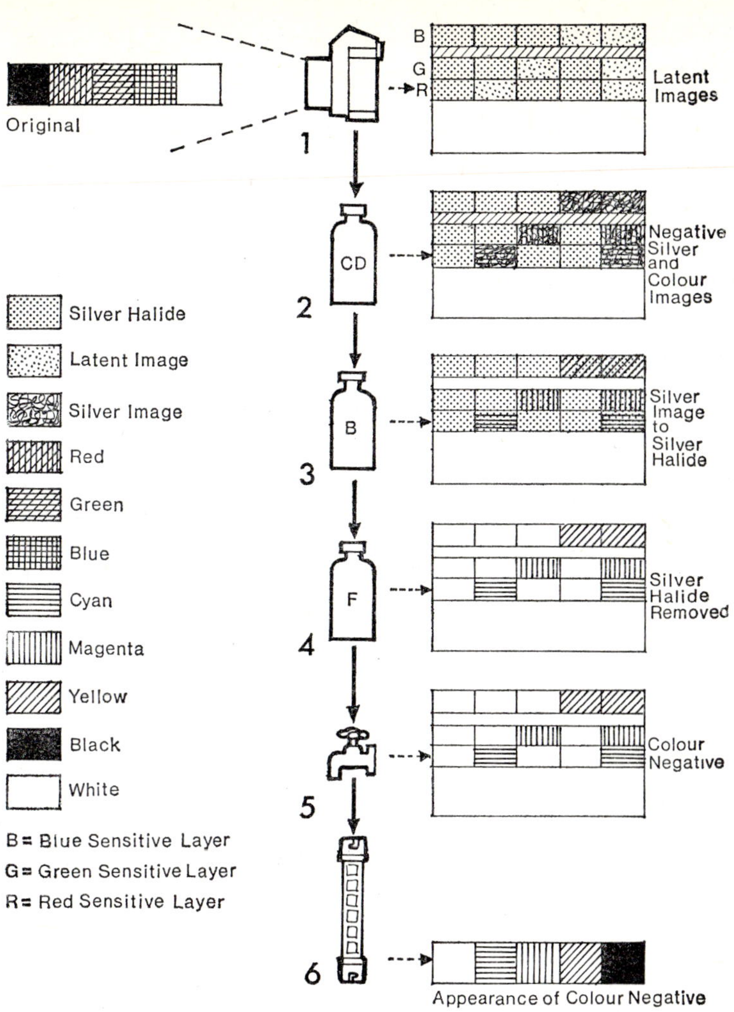

Formation of a colour negative. 1, Exposure forms a latent image. 2, Colour developer produces silver and dye images. 3, Bleach converts silver to silver bromide. 4, 5, Fixing and washing removes silver bromide and unexposed silver halide. 6, Colour negative shows reversed tones and hues of original.

from the white light and thus create red. All other colours and colour mixtures of the original are similarly reproduced.

Processing colour negative films

The processing of colour negative films is very little different from processing black-and-white films. The main differences are that in colour processing a dye image is formed together with the black silver image during the colour development stage, and that this silver image is not required and is subsequently removed by bleach and fixing stages.

The basic steps involved in processing a typical colour negative film are as follows:

1 Colour development, which forms a dye image together with a silver image.
2 Bleach, which converts the silver image to a silver halide (silver bromide) which can then be removed by the fixer.
3 Fix, to remove both the unexposed silver halide and the silver halide formed by the bleach.
4 Wash, to remove unwanted chemicals.
5 Dry.

Some processes combine the bleach and fixing steps in a single bleach-fix solution. This reduces the process to just the same number of steps as black-and-white development.

Processing colour reversal films

There are appropriate kits available for processing most types of colour reversal film at home. This is the most complex type of processing, but provided the manufacturer's instructions are carefully followed it is no more difficult to carry out than black-and-white processing.

Like colour negative films, colour reversal films are integral tripacks but, as no printing stage is involved, they contain no masking layer. Such a mask would, in any case, obscure the true colours of the scene and make the transparency unsuitable for viewing.

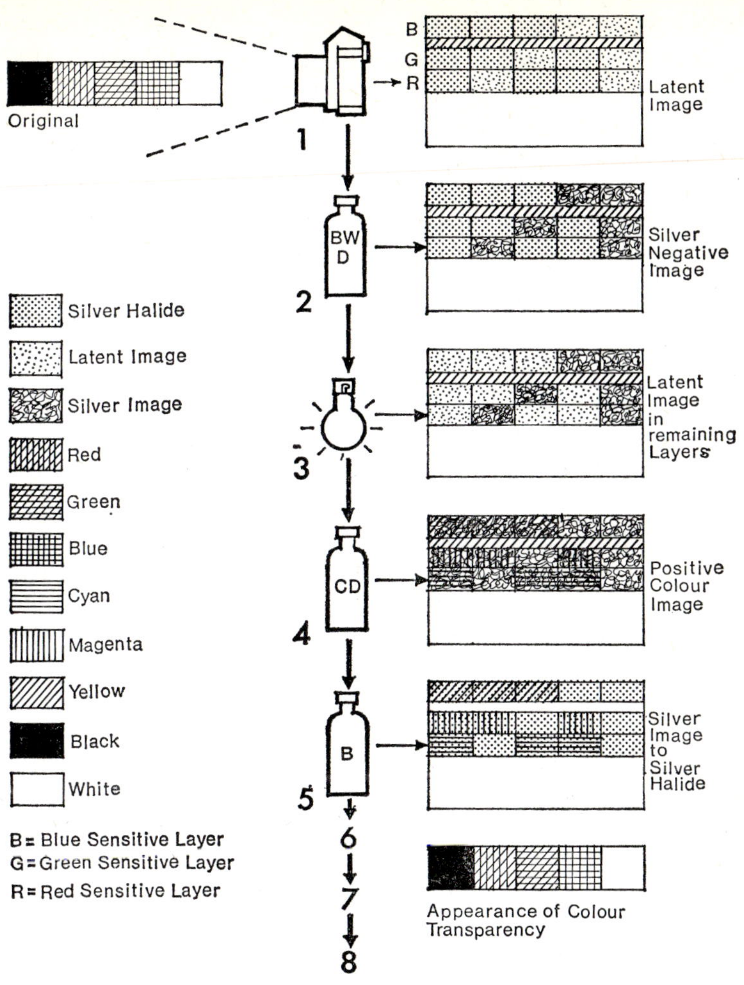

Formation of colour transparency. 1, Exposure forms latent negative image. 2, First development produces unstable negative image. 3, Re-exposure produces latent positive image. 4, Colour development produces silver and dye positive image. 5,6, Bleach and fixer remove silver image, leaving positive dye image. 7,8, Washing and drying provide transparency with colours of original.

Processing follows the general scheme used for the reversal processing of black-and-white films, but the silver image is removed because the final image must consist only of dyes. The general method is to develop the film in a black-and-white developer to form negative silver images in the three layers. The remainder of the emulsion is next exposed and then colour developed to form the positive dye image together with the corresponding positive silver image. The positive and negative silver images formed during the black-and-white and the colour development stages are then removed by bleaching, followed by fixing. Finally, the unwanted chemicals are removed by washing, and drying yields a positive colour transparency which can be viewed immediately.

The principles that apply to the formation of a colour print also apply to the formation of a colour transparency and the 'colour equations' may be used to explain the reproduction of the particular colour. For example, consider the reproduction of a red colour by a colour reversal film. On exposing the film in the camera, a latent image is formed in the red-sensitive layer. The first development step results in development of this latent image to form a silver image. Exposing the film to white light (or the use of a colour developer containing a chemical fogging agent, see page 136) causes the originally unexposed blue and green sensitive layers to be rendered developable. Development in a colour developer, followed by bleaching, fixing, etc., results in the formation of yellow and magenta dye images which, as can be seen from the 'colour equations', appear red: i.e. white light minus blue and minus green.

Processing colour prints

Colour prints obtained from colour negatives are processed by a similar procedure to that used for colour negatives but is simplified by combining the action of bleaching and fixing in a single solution termed a *bleach-fix* or *blix*. Thus only two basic solutions are used and the processing procedure is almost as easy as that used for processing black-and-white prints. The main differences being that processing times are longer and the control of temperature is more critical.

The basic steps involved in processing colour prints obtained from printing colour negatives may be summarized as follows:

1 Colour development to form a dye image together with a silver image.
2 Bleach-fix to remove the unwanted silver image and any unexposed silver halide.
3 Wash to remove chemicals.
4 Stabilize (now becoming optional) to harden the emulsion, make the image more stable and aid even drying.
5 Dry.

Colour prints may be obtained from colour slides, either by using a reversal paper and a similar processing procedure to that described earlier for processing colour reversal films, or by the Cibachrome process in which dyes (cyan, magenta and yellow) already present in the coated material are bleached, during processing, in proportion to the amount of silver formed on exposure and development. The processing sequence for Cibachrome-A is as follows:

1 Development to form a negative silver image.
2 Bleach to remove the dyes in proportion to the amount of silver and to convert the silver to silver halide.
3 Fix to remove unexposed silver halide and that converted in the bleach.
4 Wash to remove chemicals.
5 Dry.

Quality obtainable

Provided that the film has been correctly exposed and the manufacturer's processing instructions are adhered to, 'perfect' results can be obtained each time. However, mistakes can and do occur, even with the most careful of workers. The types of defects most commonly encountered, together with any means of rectifying them, are listed in a later chapter. Handling faults such as scratches, blemishes, finger marks, etc., which unfortunately are not uncommon when films are sent away for processing, can be avoided completely with home processing.

Your films can be given individual and careful treatment and are not part of a production-line method.

It is rather difficult to define exactly what is meant by 'perfect' results. With black-and-white negatives, a correctly exposed and developed negative should show some detail even in the lightest parts *(shadow areas).* The most dense parts *(highlights)* should also show some detail and not be completely black. The simplest way to check this is to lay the negative on a printed page such as this and look at it in good light. You should just be able to see printing through the dark areas of the negative. Small deviations from the ideal negative can be overcome at the printing stage and larger deviations from this ideal case can be corrected by a chemical treatment such as *intensification* or *reduction* (see page 191).

With a colour negative, however, its visual appearance is no criterion of acceptability. A colour negative is considered acceptable if it yields a good colour reproduction when printed. The printing stage in colour reproduction can accommodate only a very limited deviation from a good colour negative and no chemical treatment is possible to correct for processing faults. However, as you shall see later on, colour negatives are processed by a more uniform procedure than black-and-white negatives, and variations in the negative are due mainly to exposure errors rather than processing variations.

In general, correctly exposed and processed negatives or positives should give positives of a correct and natural scale of brightness from the deepest shadows to the highlights. In the case of colour materials, the reproduction of colours should also appear natural from the shadows to the highlights. Although perfect reproduction of colour is not possible, colour prints or transparencies should appear natural and be free from colour casts. The prime aims are generally that greys should reproduce as greys and that flesh tones should look normal. If these aims are achieved, then slight imperfections in the reproduction of other colours are acceptable.

These expected results may sound formidable and difficult to achieve, but processing is the easiest part of photography, in which excellent results can be achieved by following a simple routine.

Darkroom Facilities and Equipment

For home-processing of films a darkroom is not essential because daylight-loading tanks are available, or darkroom-loading tanks may be used in conjunction with a changing bag. Also, darkroom-loading tanks may be loaded in any room that can be temporarily blacked out for the short period of time required for the loading operation.
Converting an existing room to a darkroom usually involves stopping light coming in through the windows. This can be achieved by temporarily covering the window with an opaque material such as black polythene sheeting or hardboard. If light coming in around the door is a problem, then fitting any proprietary draught-excluder should be an effective remedy.

Improvising a darkroom

Although loading of developing tanks can be carried out using a changing bag or in a room that is temporarily blacked out, it is convenient if a somewhat more permanent darkroom and workroom can be improvised. It is worthwhile considering the construction of a darkroom at this stage because, if you are interested in processing negative films, you will almost certainly want to extend your home-processing activities to printing your negatives. An improvised darkroom, if designed properly, can also serve as a workroom in which loading of tanks, film processing, enlarging and print-processing can all be undertaken.
The obvious choice for such a room is the bathroom, which is equipped with hot and cold running water and normally has only a small window requiring blacking out. Also, it is one of the few rooms in the house that is little used. A wooden top can easily be made to fit over the bath to form a working surface, or alternatively a slightly more sophisticated arrangement can be used which has a vertical partition to separate the working area into wet and dry sections. The dry section, furthest from the taps is a convenient place to load the tank, while the wet area nearest the taps is ideal for carrying out processing. A wooden sink or trough, lined with polythene sheeting or painted with a waterproof paint, can be constructed and

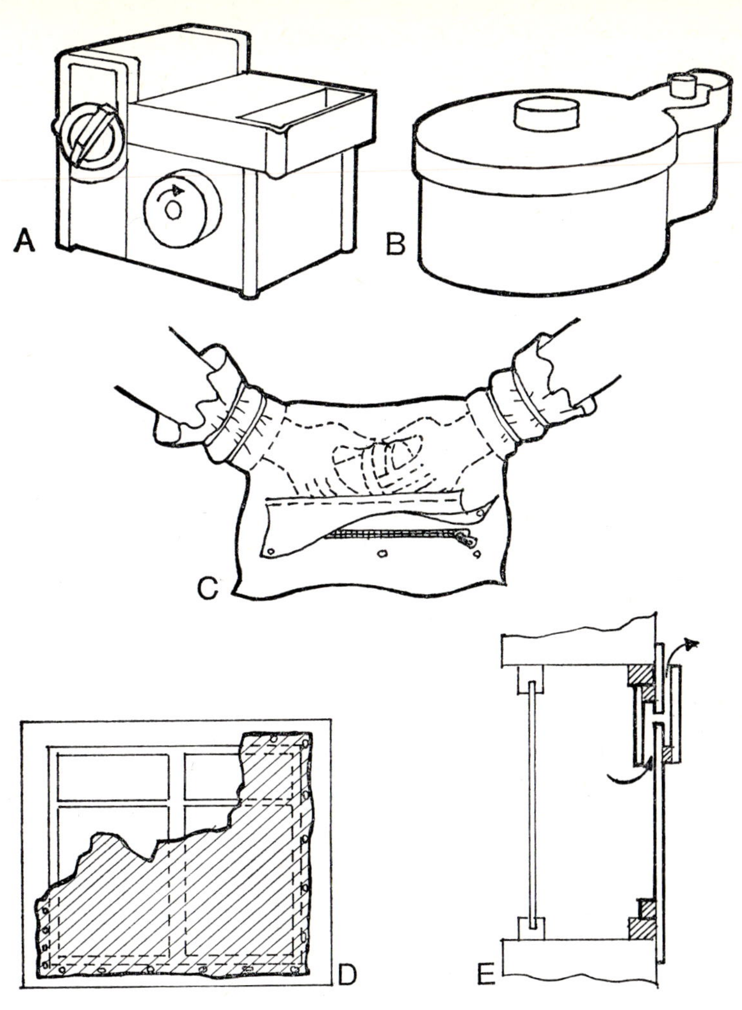

A, B. Daylight loading developing tanks. **C,** A changing bag allows sensitised materials to be handled without a darkroom. **D,** Blackout with opaque plastic sheeting. **E,** Method of light-trapped ventilation.

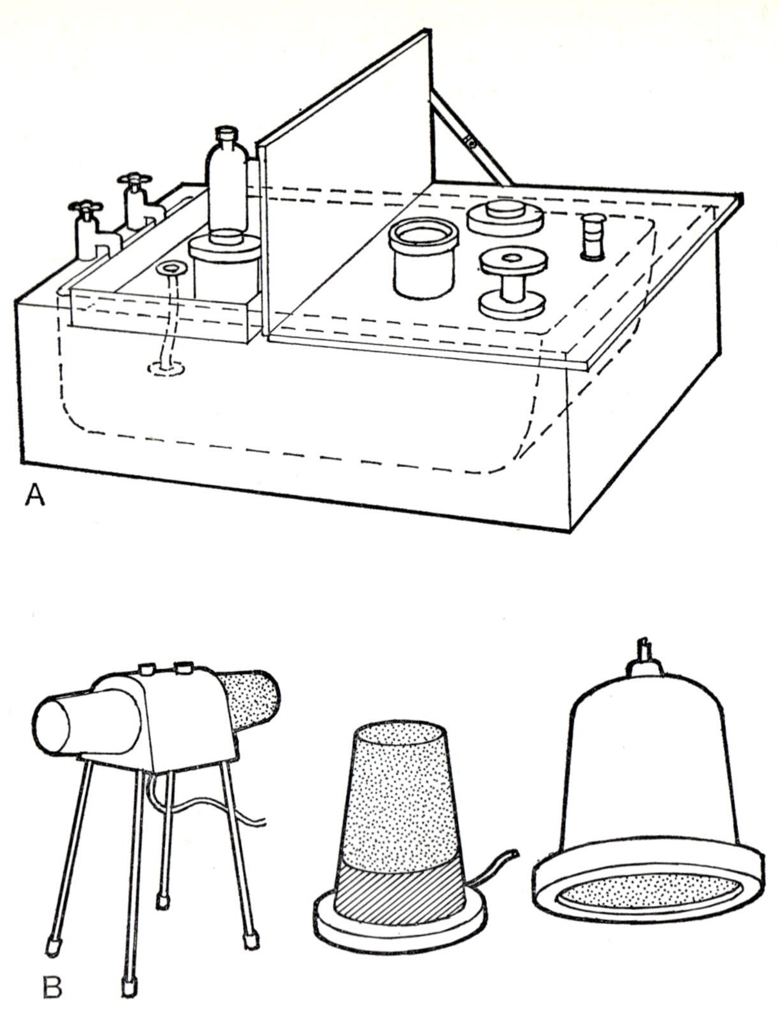

A, Possible construction of a working area on a bath top. The section nearer the taps is the wet area for processing – in a water bath if necessary. The other side of the partition can be used for tank loading and/or enlarging. **B,** Forms of amateur safelight.

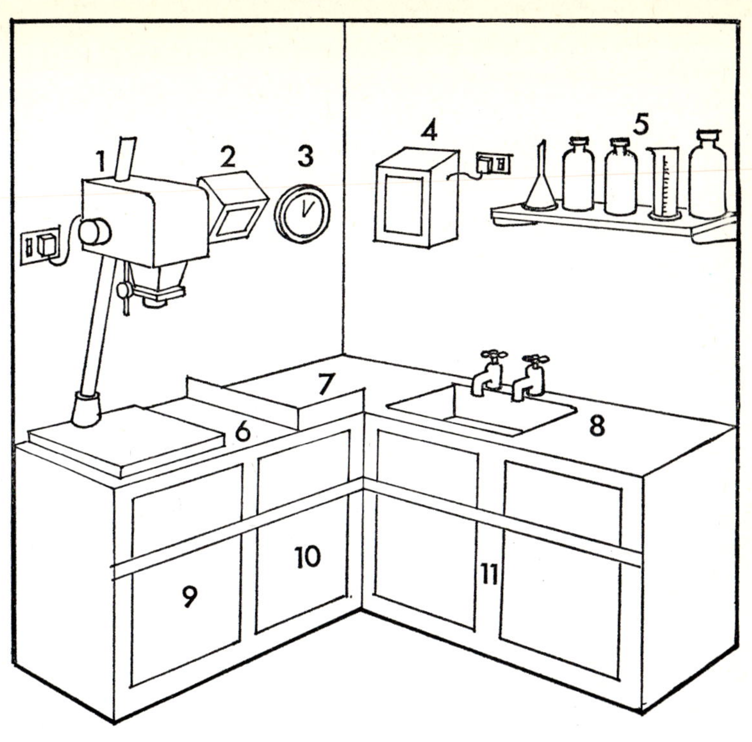

Layout for permanent darkroom about 6 × 6 × 8ft. 1, Enlarger. 2, Safelight. 3, Timer. 4, Viewing box. 5, Solutions, etc. 6, Dry area for printing, etc. 7,8, Wet area with sink and draining surface. 9,10, Storage for papers, films, etc. 11, Storage for dishes, tanks, etc.

preferably fitted with a waste pipe and a flexible tube leading into the bath waste pipe. Fitting of a waste pipe to the trough avoids splashing the bath with chemicals when they are discarded, and the trough can also serve as a constant temperature bath if the room temperature is different from the required processing temperature.

The blacking out of the windows is a relatively easy matter, (see page 31) and ideally a blackout with ventilation should be used, especially if the bathroom is small and long stays are envisaged.

This simple arrangement can be adapted readily at a later date for printing negatives by placing the enlarger in the dry section and the processing dishes in the wet area nearest the taps. For printing negatives, some illumination will be required in the room. Photographic suppliers sell safelights of various shapes and sizes. These are lamps usually of 15 or 25 watts enclosed in a box containing an appropriate filter such that the light emitted will not fog the material being used. Typically, these are orange or olive green for bromide enlarging papers and amber or dark green for colour printing papers. Recommendations for the appropriate safelight filter will almost certainly be provided by the paper or safelight manufacturer, and if there is any doubt as to the suitability of your particular safelight for the printing paper being used, it is best to follow the paper manufacturer's recommendations.

Layout for permanent darkroom

Ideally, a separate room should be set aside as a darkroom, but few of us are in the happy position of having a room which can be used exclusively for photographic work. If this should prove possible, then a proper purpose-built professional type darkroom can be constructed, using built-in kitchen furniture, which is now readily available in assemble-yourself kits.

A suggestion for such a layout is given in the diagram on page 33 for a small room measuring approximately 6 × 6 × 8 ft. Exact measurements, of course, will depend on the size of room available and positioning of doors and windows, but the basic principle is to separate the dry working area and storage facilities from the wet working area and storage facilities. The diagram on page 33 represents a professional approach to darkroom layout for enlarging and processing negatives and prints, but will be beyond the reach of most amateurs who will have to use an improvised darkroom layout of the type shown on page 32. More specific details of the design and construction of purpose-built professional darkrooms are to be found in the manufacturers' data books or more specialised books which cover enlarging in greater detail.

Processing equipment

In order to process your own films, you will require the items listed below. The list represents simple, basic and inexpensive equipment which can be added to as the home-processor sees fit.

1. A developing tank in which the processing is carried out.
2. Measuring cylinders or graduated beakers in appropriate sizes for accurately measuring volumes of solutions.
3. A beaker or two in which powdered chemicals can be dissolved.
4. A stirring rod for mixing chemicals.
5. A funnel for transferring solutions to bottles.
6. A selection of bottles for storing processing solutions.
7. A thermometer for measuring solution temperatures.
8. A clock or stop-watch for timing processing.
9. Clips for hanging films up to dry.
10. A changing bag, if required.
11. Miscellaneous items such as a rag for wiping up any spilt solutions, a short length of flexible tubing for attaching to a tap (see page 79), film wiper (see page 82), and a bowl for standing the developing tank in (see page 74).

The list of equipment can be shortened, depending on the type of process and chemicals to be used. Thus, concentrated liquid stock solutions only require dilution with a specified volume of water before use, so items 3–6 need not be obtained. Certain items, such as the clock, are available in most households,

while the changing bag is needed only if a darkroom-loading developing tank is used and no darkroom is available.
Some manufacturers of photographic equipment offer processing kits which contain everything necessary for the amateur to process his own films. These are to be recommended as a way of introducing the novice to the enjoyment of home-processing
If, however, you are thinking of buying individual items to equip your own processing laboratory, buy only from specialist photographic firms and do not 'make do' with substitute items from hardware shops. Equipment sold by specialist photographic firms is suitable for use with photographic chemicals, whereas general kitchen equipment may be affected by such chemicals or may contaminate processing solutions.

Developing tanks

Modern developing tanks are constructed of plastic or stainless steel and contain a reel or spiral on which the film is wound. The film is held in position and separated by a spiral guide which ensures that processing solutions can freely and evenly circulate around the film. Developing tanks may conveniently be divided into two types: darkroom-loading and daylight-loading.
The most common and inexpensive developing tank is the darkroom-loading type which, after loading in a darkroom or changing bag, is used in normal lighting conditions. These tanks are suitably light-trapped so that solutions can be poured in and out without light getting in; they are self-contained miniature darkrooms.
Many different designs are available in a multiplicity of sizes. Some have a fixed spiral and are suitable for processing one film size only, whilst others contain an adjustable spiral and can be used to process film sizes of 35 mm, 126, 127 and 120/220. Apart from the relative cost and a decision on appropriate tank size, the ease of loading the film on the particular spiral is a very important consideration. This can only be found out by a practical test, preferably in the dark.

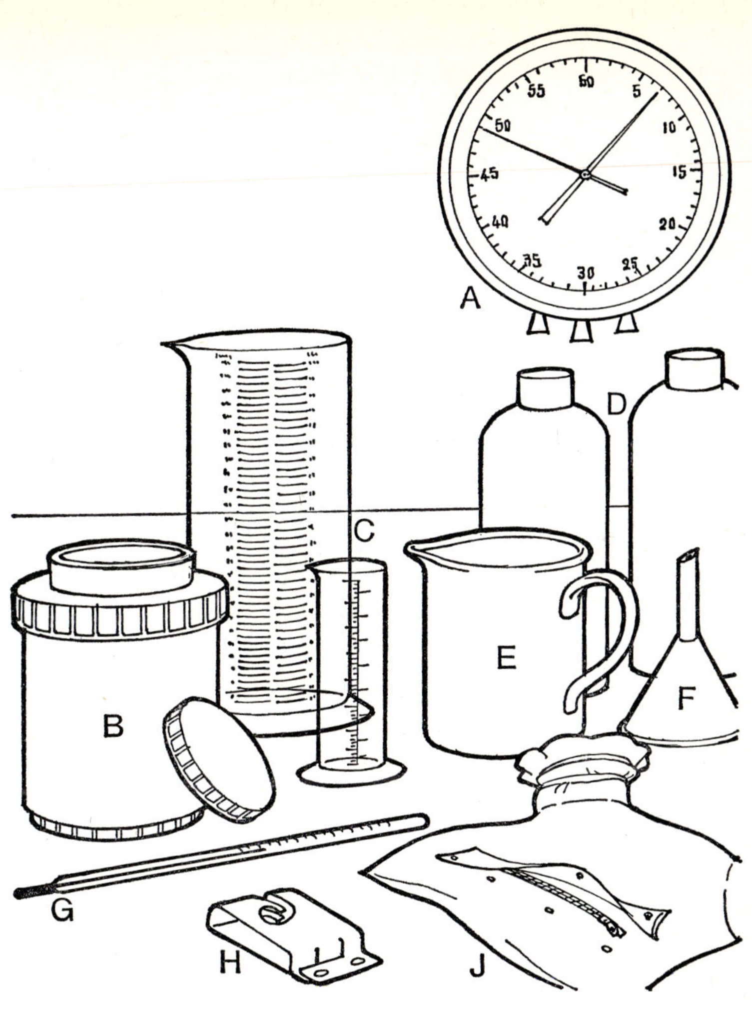

Processing equipment. **A,** Timer. **B**, Developing tank. **C,** Graduated measures. **D,** Storage bottles. **E,** Jug. **F,** Funnel. **G,** Thermometer. **H,** Film clip. **J,** Changing bag.

Three types of spiral are commonly available:

1 *Self-loading,* in which the film is pushed into the entry point of the outer groove and the two halves are then rotated backwards and forwards. The film is drawn into the spiral by a ball-bearing or similar mechanism that alternatively grips and releases the edge of the film.
2 *Centre-loading,* with a spring clip on the central core which holds the end of the film securely. The film is loaded from the centre of the spiral outwards by rotating the spiral in one direction.
3 *Automatic-loading* spirals are adaptations of the centre-load spirals, in which a guide is used to aid introduction of the film into the groove.

Daylight-loading tanks, although less common than the dark-room-loading types, are also available. As their name signifies, these tanks do not require any darkroom whatsoever and all operations from loading to processing can be undertaken in the light. They are, however, more expensive than the darkroom-loading tanks because of their more complicated construction. A typical daylight-loading 35 mm developing tank contains a separate compartment in which the cassette is placed. The film is guided to the centre of the spiral, where it is held by a clip. After closing the lid, the film is wound on to the spiral by rotating a knob on the outside of the tank. When the film is fully wound on to the spiral, it is cut from the cassette spool by a knife built into the tank body.

Essentially similar tanks are used for 120 size films, except that after placing the film spool in the side chamber the end of the backing paper is threaded through a slot at the side. The lid is then closed and the backing paper gently withdrawn through the slot. This causes the film to unwind from the spool through a second slot into the tank body, where it slides into the grooves of a spiral reel.

Measures and containers

Measuring cylinders (or graduated beakers) are made of glass or suitable plastic material such as polystyrene or polythene.

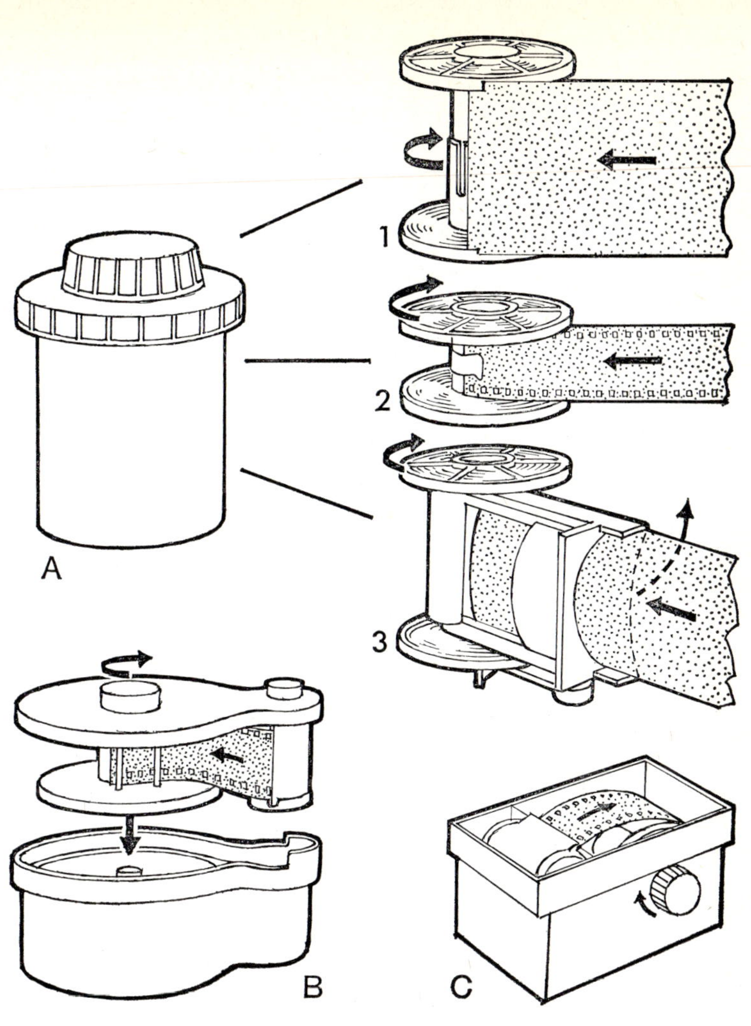

Developing tanks and spirals. **A,** Developing tank, which may be used with **1**, self-loading spiral. 2, centre-loading spiral. **3**, automatic loading spiral. **B,C,** daylight-loading tanks.

For amateur use, plastic vessels are recommended because of their strength and cheapness in comparison with the somewhat more expensive and less robust glass vessels.

You will require at least one measuring cylinder or graduated beaker of sufficient capacity to measure the largest volume of solution that you are preparing. One litre or 500 ml are the usual sizes. Also, one or more smaller, more accurate cylinders of either 50 ml or 25 ml capacity with divisions of 1 ml will be required for accurately measuring small volumes of solutions.

If powdered chemicals are to be dissolved then a beaker or two will be needed, although wide measuring cylinders or graduated beakers may serve the dual function of beaker and measure.

To increase the rate of dissolution of powdered chemicals and to aid the mixing of concentrated solutions with water, a stirrer should be used. This can be a simple glass or plastic rod. A stainless steel spoon reserved exclusively for use with photographic chemicals is equally suitable. Avoid using wooden rods, because they tend to absorb chemicals and are difficult to clean

A funnel of appropriate size is useful for transferring solutions from beakers or measuring cylinders to bottles without spillage. Make sure that the funnel that you buy has external ribs, to prevent air seals being formed with the neck of the bottle and to allow rapid transfer of solutions.

For storage of stock solutions of processing chemicals, a selection of bottles is needed. Brown glass bottles are the most suitable for storage of developers, because they are easily cleaned and their dark colour reduces the possibility of light-induced chemical reactions on the contents.

Polythene bottles are suitable for storage of other processing solutions, but on no account store processing solutions in discarded soft drink or beer bottles. This could lead to confusion, with disastrous results!

Thermometers and clocks

The rate at which chemical reactions such as development occur is affected by temperature. It is, therefore, of the utmost importance to measure and accurately control the temperature

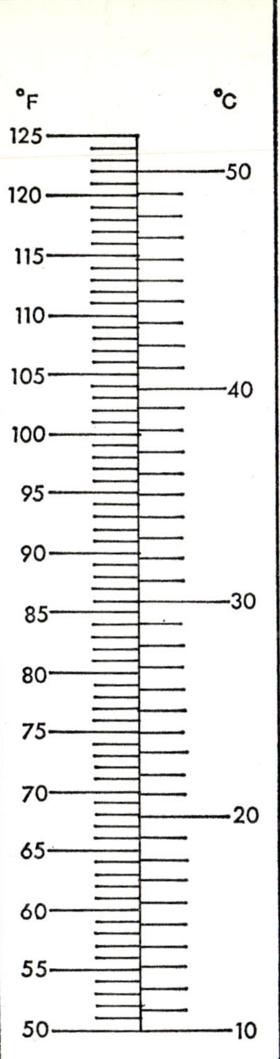

Conversion of degrees Fahrenheit to degrees Centigrade or Celsius. The conversion formula is °C = (°F–32)5/9.

of processing solutions in order to achieve reproducible results. A spirit-filled thermometer accurate to $\pm\frac{1}{2}$°C is suitable for black-and-white processing, but for colour processing it is usually necessary to control tne temperature to within $\pm\frac{1}{4}$°C and a more accurate mercury-filled thermometer is required. Black-and-white processing is commonly carried out at around 20°C (68°F). Colour processes, though, often take place at temperatures up to 40°C (104°F). So, for both types, you need a thermometer that covers this range – say 10–50°C or 50–125°F. Processing is not only temperature dependent, but is also time dependent. The watch or clock used does not have to be an accurate timekeeper in the general sense of the word, but it must be consistent, so that a given setting or interval always represents the same duration. to within about five seconds.

Film clips

After processing, the film must be dried. The simplest method of drying is to hang the film in a convenient place. Stainless steel film clips especially designed for this purpose are sold by most photographic retailers, although wooden or plastic clothes pegs can be used, provided that they grip the film securely. A weighted clip should be attached to the bottom of the film to prevent it curling while drying.

Changing bag

When a darkroom-loading tank is used in the absence of darkroom facilities, a changing bag is needed. Changing bags are made from a thick light-tight material and are usually fitted with a zip-fastener for ease of introduction of the film and developing tank. Two armholes are provided, which are fitted with elasticated cuffs to ensure a snug fit over the arms.
It is best to use the changing bag while sitting at a table, with the bag and its contents resting on the table in front of you just as if you were loading a tank in a darkened room. A disadvantage of using a changing bag is that it rests on top of your

hands while you are working, which makes manipulations more difficult. Also, changing bags are almost airtight as well as light-tight, and your hands may become damp with perspiration, which makes manipulations still harder and may cause finger marks on the film you are handling.

Preparation of Solutions and General Technique

The main requirement for the preparation of processing solutions is *cleanliness.* All beakers, bottles, measuring cylinders, etc., must be scrupulously clean. Always wash apparatus thoroughly immediately after you have used it. Not only is it then easier to clean, but the possibility of contamination of one solution with another is avoided.

Faults in processing are often caused by contamination of solutions during their preparation. If possible, reserve one mixing vessel for use with only one type of solution, and if several solutions are to be mixed, prepare them in the order in which they are going to be used. This will reduce still further the likelihood of one of the more serious causes of contamination – namely, traces of fixer in developer, which can cause serious fogging, whereas traces of developer in a fixer have little or no effect on the results.

All equipment needed for preparation of processing solutions should be laid out before starting, so that each item is at hand when required. It is advisable to mix all processing solutions in a different place from where the film is to be loaded and away from foodstuffs and furniture in case solutions are spilt. It is important to avoid all contact of processing solutions with hands, clothing, etc., and if you inadvertently come into contact with processing solutions, wash thoroughly with water. Avoidance of contact with processing solutions is especially important in colour processing, because many of these solutions contain allergenic or toxic chemicals. Rubber gloves should be worn when preparing processing solutions, as an added precaution.

Preparing developer solutions

There are many proprietary developers on the market which have been designed especially for the home-processor. They have been formulated for ease of preparation of working solutions as well as for achieving the desired photographic results. Developers are available as either concentrated solutions or powders.

The preparation of a working strength developer from a

concentrated solution is simplicity itself. Generally, the liquid concentrate is accompanied by an instruction such as 'dilute 1+9', or some similar statement. This means that one part by volume of the concentrated developer is to be diluted with nine parts by volume of water. Unless instructed otherwise, tap water is suitable for the preparation of developers.

In order to dilute the concentrated developer to the working solution strength, you must first find out the minimum volume of solution needed to process your film size in your developing tank (this figure is normally moulded into the lid or body of the developing tank). If, for example, this figure is 300 ml, then 30 ml of the concentrated developer must be diluted with 270 ml of water.

For ease of calculation of other volumes and dilutions different from the above example, a general formula can be written:

For instruction: 'dilute 1+v' (1 part by volume of developer and v parts by volume of water).

Then: $1x+vx=V$

or $$x=\frac{V}{1+v}$$

where V is the total volume or tank capacity and x is the factor for working out quantities of developer and water required (1x and vx respectively).

For the example already given:

$$v=9 \text{ ml}$$
$$V=300 \text{ ml}$$

$$x=\frac{300}{1+9}=\frac{300}{10}=30$$

Thus, we require 1×30 or 30 ml of concentrated developer and 9×30 or 270 ml of water.

If the total volume needed is only 250 ml:

$$v=9 \text{ ml}$$
$$V=250 \text{ ml}$$

$$x=\frac{250}{1+9}=\frac{250}{10}=25$$

Thus, we now require 1×25 or 25 ml of concentrated developer and 9×25 or 225 ml of water.

Without too much difficulty, this simple calculation can be used for working out quantities required for any dilution and any total volume. The calculation also applies to other units of volume such as fluid ounces.
Once you have worked out the volumes of concentrated developer and water that you need for your particular film size and tank, proceed as follows:

1 Three-quarters fill a graduated beaker or measuring cylinder, large enough to hold the final volume, with cold tap water. This volume is not critical and need not be accurately measured.
2 Add sufficient hot water to bring the temperature a degree or two above the development temperature, i.e. 70°F or 21°C if the development temperature is 68°F or 20°C.
3 Pour out sufficient water until exactly the calculated volume of water remains.
4 Pour the calculated volume of concentrated developer into a small accurate measure.
5 Add the developer to the water.

The developer is now diluted to the working strength and is ready for use (see page 72). The developer should also be at the correct temperature for processing.
Powdered developers are slightly less convenient to use than concentrated liquid developers; usually, there are the contents of two packets to dissolve, and dissolving a solid takes longer than diluting a concentrated solution. Also, many of the powdered developers require the preparation of a stock solution which, in turn, requires diluting to prepare the working strength solution. This increases the number of manipulations before developing can be started. This slight drawback is, however, partially offset by their lower cost than the concentrated solutions.
For the preparation of developers from powdered chemicals, carefully follow the instructions provided by the supplier. Never take a small quantity from the packet to make up a smaller volume of solution than the entire packet would make. There are many ingredients (see page 64) in the packet and they may not be uniformly distributed. Solutions may therefore

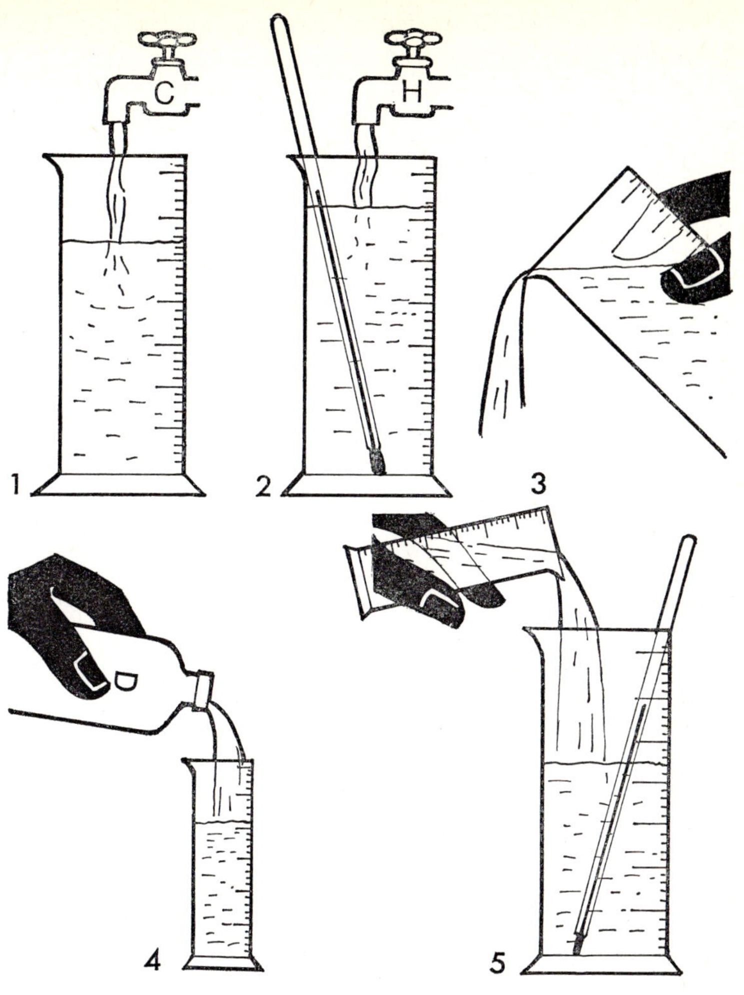

Preparation of working strength developer from stock solution. 1, Three-quarters fill with cold water a measure large enough to hold the required volume. 2, Add hot water until the solution is a degree or two above working temperature. 3, Pour out water until exactly the required quantity remains. 4, Measure out the appropriate quantity of stock solution. 5, Add stock solution to water.

vary in composition when small portions are removed from the packet.

The general procedure for dissolving powdered developers may be summarised as follows:

1 Into a graduated beaker or wide measuring cylinder of sufficient capacity, pour approximately three-quarters of the recommended volume of warm water at a temperature not greater than 125°F or 50°C.
2 Add the contents of the first packet slowly while stirring. Stir until *completely* dissolved.
3 Add the contents of the second packet and stir until this also has completely dissolved.
4 Make up to the recommended volume by adding cold water.

The developer is now ready for use and should be at approximately the correct temperature. If not, it can be cooled by standing the beaker in a basin of cold water. If the developer so prepared is a stock solution, it can be poured into a bottle of appropriate size for storage (see page 52) and the working strength solution can be prepared by following the dilution procedure given earlier for concentrated liquid developers.

During the mixing of powdered developers, proper agitation is essential to increase the rate at which the chemicals dissolve. It is important to ensure that agitation is not too vigorous or air may be drawn into the developer solution and cause *oxidation* of the developing agent (see page 53). The effect of this is a decrease in developer activity, a colouration of the solution and the likelihood of staining. For similar reasons, care should be exercised when transferring developers to bottles or developing tanks. This should be done slowly and smoothly, so that little, if any, air is drawn in with the solution.

Preparing other solutions

The preparation of fixers is carried out in a similar way to developers, except that concentrations are not quite so critical and aerial oxidation is not significant.

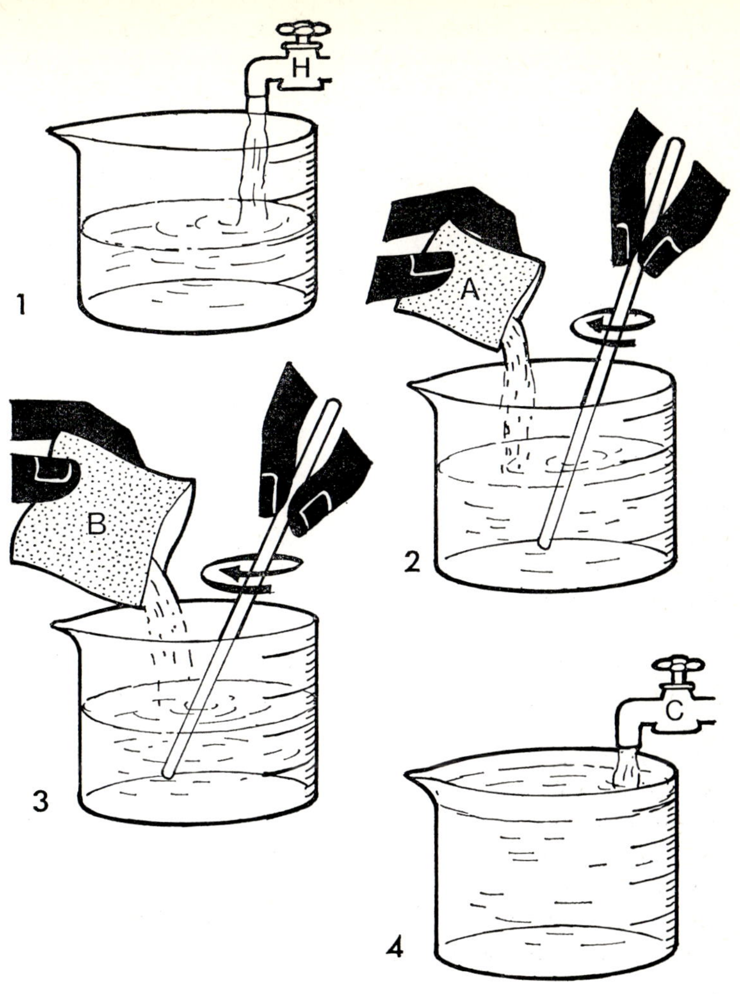

Preparation of developer solution from powdered chemicals. 1, Pour about three-quarters of the required volume of water into a measure at about 125°F (50°C). 2, Add contents of smaller packet (**A**), stirring until completely dissolved. 3, Add contents of larger packet (**B**) slowly, stirring until dissolved. 4, Make up to correct volume with cold water.

Like developers, fixers are available as concentrated solutions or powders. The main difference in the preparation of fixer solutions is that, on dissolving, the solution tends to get very cold. Hot water is generally recommended for their preparation, unless instructed otherwise. Temperature recommendations for dissolving fixers should always be followed because, with some fixer formulations, decomposition and precipitation of the ingredients may occur if their maximum temperature of dissolution is exceeded.

Some processing solutions, notably stop baths, may call for a 3% solution of acetic acid, for example. For a liquid such as acetic acid this means that 3 parts by volume of the liquid should be made *up to* 100 parts by volume with the solvent (usually water). For a solid, 3 parts by weight of the solid are dissolved in a small volume and the solution made *up to* 100 parts by volume.

The general principles of dissolving and diluting chemicals are given under developers, and these general principles apply to all processing solutions, whether they be for black-and-white or colour processing. Suppliers of photographic chemicals provide specific instructions for the preparation of solutions, and these instructions should be carefully followed because they represent the optimum conditions found from many years of practical experience.

Neither be tempted to speed up the dissolving or mixing of chemicals by using higher temperatures than those recommended, nor rush the procedure by adding all the constituents in one go. Care in the preparation and handling of solutions will reap benefits in the excellent results that you will obtain when you use the solutions.

Storage of processing solutions

Most processing solutions for black-and-white materials will keep for months if stored correctly, whereas colour processing solutions are generally much less stable and may only keep for weeks. Air and extremes in temperature are the major enemies of processing solutions, especially developers. Oxidation of a developer may take place even in a tightly sealed bottle if the solution level is low and there is a large air gap. It is, therefore advisable to store developers in bottles of such a size hat they are almost completely filled. A small air gap should be left to allow for changes in volume of the solution with temperature variations, which could cause the bottle to burst or the cap to be forced off if insufficient airspace was left.

With developer stock solutions, the air gap at the top of the bottle will increase as solution is withdrawn to prepare the working strength developer. It is better to store developer stock solutions in a number of small bottles, rather than one large bottle. This further reduces the possibility of aerial oxidation, because each small bottle would be opened a fewer number of times than one large bottle.

The temperature of storage is also important. If allowed to get too high (above 90°F or 32°C), the rate of aerial oxidation is markedly increased and decomposition of developer constituents may also occur with consequent loss in developer activity and the likelihood of staining of the processed material. If the temperature of the stored solution is allowed to drop below about 50°F or 10°C, some of the constituents may crystallise out of solution. The crystallised product may be extremely difficult, or impossible, to redissolve.

Not only should the temperature at which processing solutions are stored not be allowed to reach extremes, but they should also not be subjected to repeated fluctuations in temperature, even for short periods of time, because this also reduces the life of the solution.

Glass or polythene bottles with a tight-fitting screw cap are most convenient for storing processing solutions. Always use one bottle for storing one type of solution and never interchange bottle stoppers or caps. Contamination of one solution with another must be avoided at all costs.

The above conditions for storage have been applied to developers which are the most sensitive to variations in conditions of the solutions that you will store. These elementary precautions also apply to other processing solutions, except that in most cases aerial oxidation is less important.

Loading the developing tank

Loading tanks requires a certain minimum manipulative skill which is best acquired by practising with a dummy film in daylight. Buy the cheapest possible film of the size you are using and run it through your camera just as if you were taking photographs, then seal up the film as you would a film in normal use. Running the film through the camera is, of course, unnecessary for 35 mm film, which is rewound back into the cassette after exposing. With other film sizes the film is wound from the film spool to a take-up spool in the camera.
Before loading a film into the tank, you will have to get to the light-sensitive film itself. The way in which the film is packed to protect it from the light, when removed from the camera, varies with the film size:

TYPES OF FILM PACKING

Film size	Description of packing
35 mm (135)	Film wound on a spool in a light-tight cassette.
120	Film fixed at one end to backing paper and wound on a spool.
126, 110	As for 120 except that film and spool are contained in a cartridge.
127	As for 120.
220	Film is fixed to a paper 'leader' and 'trailer' and wound on a film spool.
620	As for 120.

Thirty-five millimetre film is wound on a spool in a cassette, which is a light-tight container with a cloth-lipped slit through which the film enters or leaves. The operations for loading a spiral are:

1 Cut off the shaped leader with a pair of scissors. Cut between the sprocket holes and not across them or jamming may occur.
2 Remove one of the ends of the cassette. The edge of a coin may be required to lever off the end of a metal cassette.
3 Remove the film from the cassette.
4 Load the film into the spiral (this is shown in detail on pages 59 and 61).

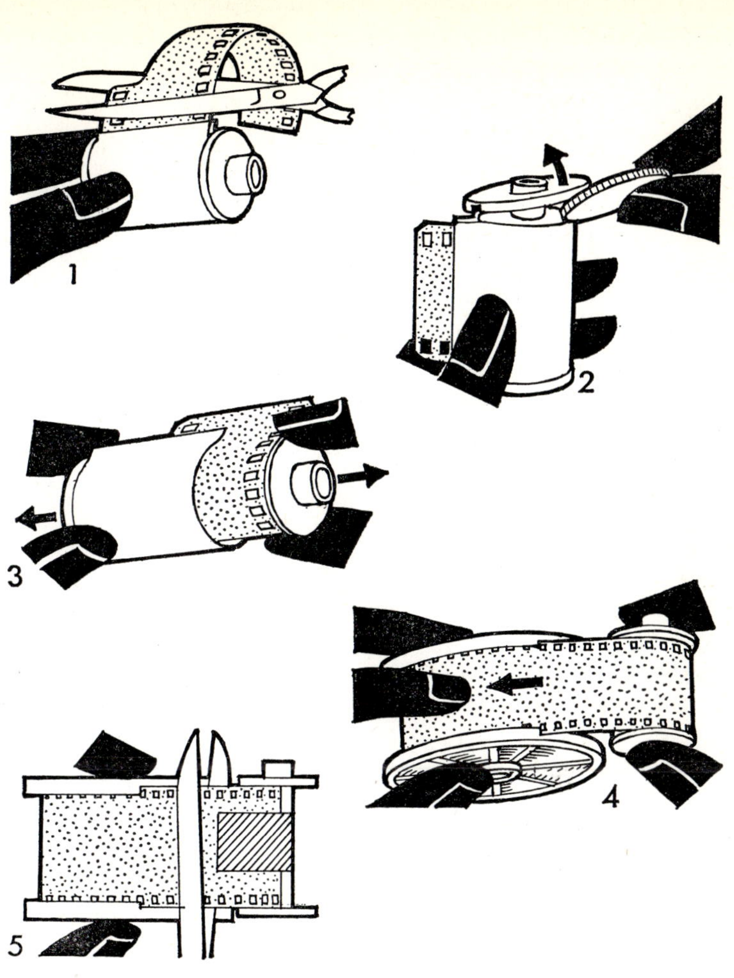

Loading a 35mm spiral. 1, Cut off the film leader between sprocket holes. 2, Remove one end from cassette in total darkness. 3, Withdraw film and spool from cassette. 4, Guide film into spiral and load. 5, Cut or tear end of film from spool.

5 When the film is fully loaded into the spiral, cut or tear the film from the spool.

With ordinary roll film, the film is attached at one end to a backing paper which is much longer than the film itself and protects it from light when tightly wound on the spool. The leading edge of the film is stuck to the backing paper with a strip of adhesive tape, but when you unroll the film after it has been through the camera you first come to the loose end. For 126 films, before getting to the roll of film you will have to break open the cartridge. This may be done as follows:

1 Firmly grip the cartridge in both hands with your fingers below the point where the larger end joins the back.
2 With your thumb on top of the larger end, sharply press down to snap off cleanly.
3 Remove pieces of the plastic cartridge from around the film, taking care not to cut yourself on any sharp pieces of plastic lying around.

The roll of film, together with its backing paper, has now been removed from the cartridge and is ready for unwinding and loading into the tank, as shown on pages 59 and 61.

No. 220 size film differs from other roll films in that it has no backing paper as such, but has a paper leader and trailer attached to each end of the film. For loading this film into the spiral, it is necessary to cut or tear off the leader, otherwise the general procedure is the same as for the other roll films.

General procedure for loading spirals

The loading of the film on the spiral has, so far, not been considered in any detail. The loading procedure does, of course, depend on the type of spiral being used. The *self-loading* spiral is widely used, and this type of spiral will be considered first. Self-loading spirals have rotating flanges and a gripping device on the outermost groove which allows the film to pass through in one direction only. Rotating the flanges backwards and forwards by a small amount causes the film to be drawn into the spiral.

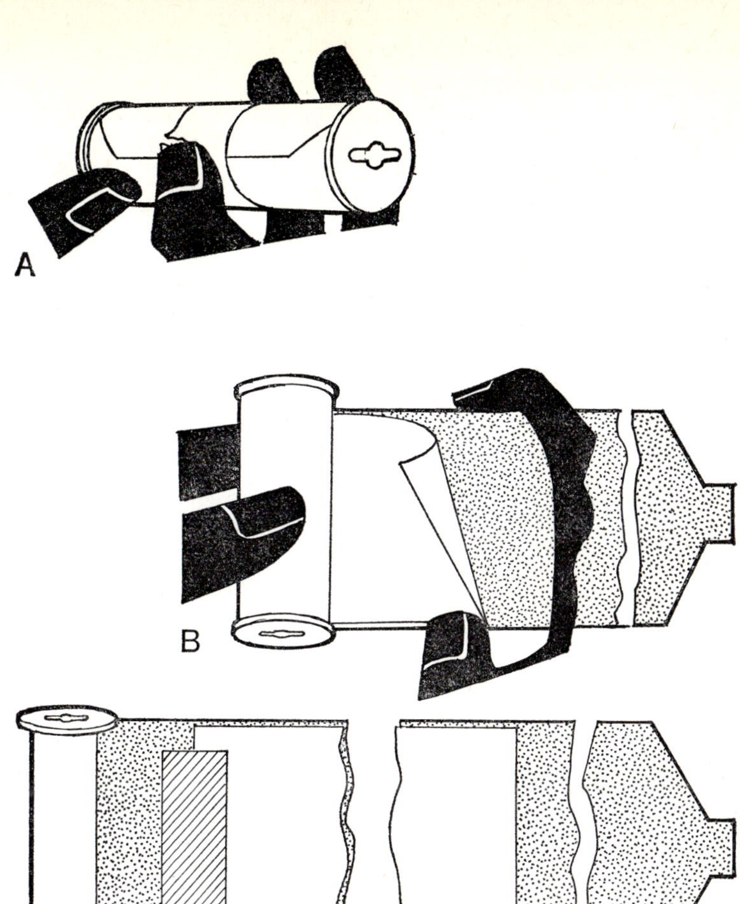

Opening roll film for processing. **A,** Remove the adhesive paper seal. **B,** Unroll the backing paper in total darkness until the film emerges. Guide film into tank and load. **C,** The end of the film is secured to the backing paper with tape and should be slowly torn off.

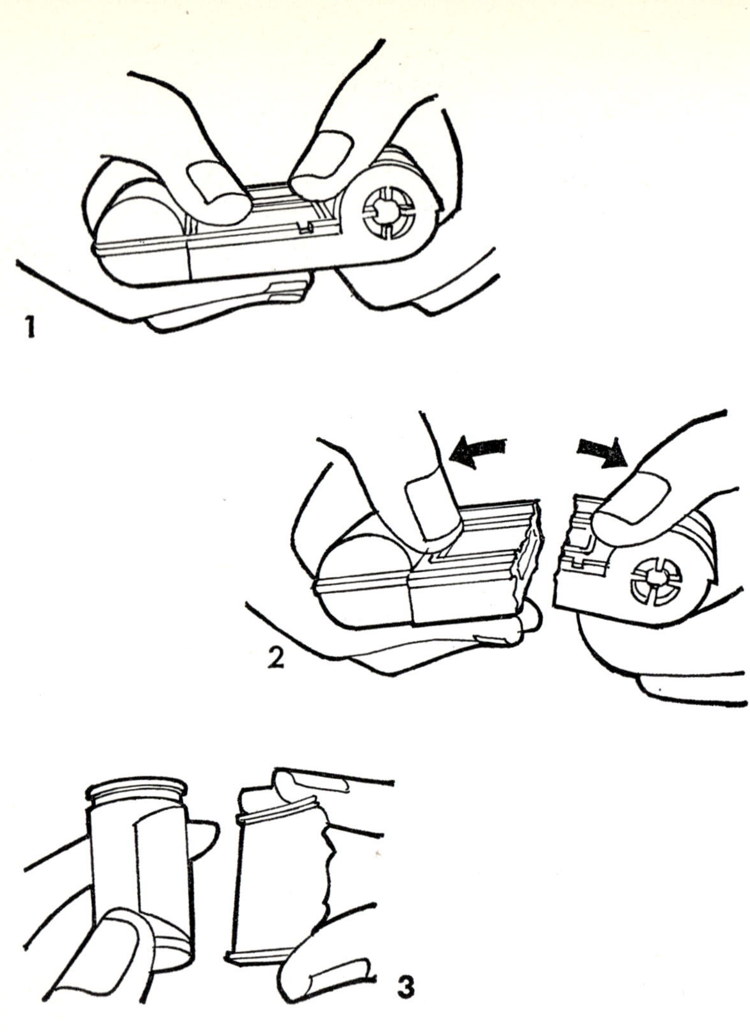

Opening a film cartridge. 1, In darkness, grip the cartridge in both hands with the fingers below the point where the larger end joins the back. 2, Sharply press down to snap the cartridge. 3, Remove the pieces of plastic from around the film.

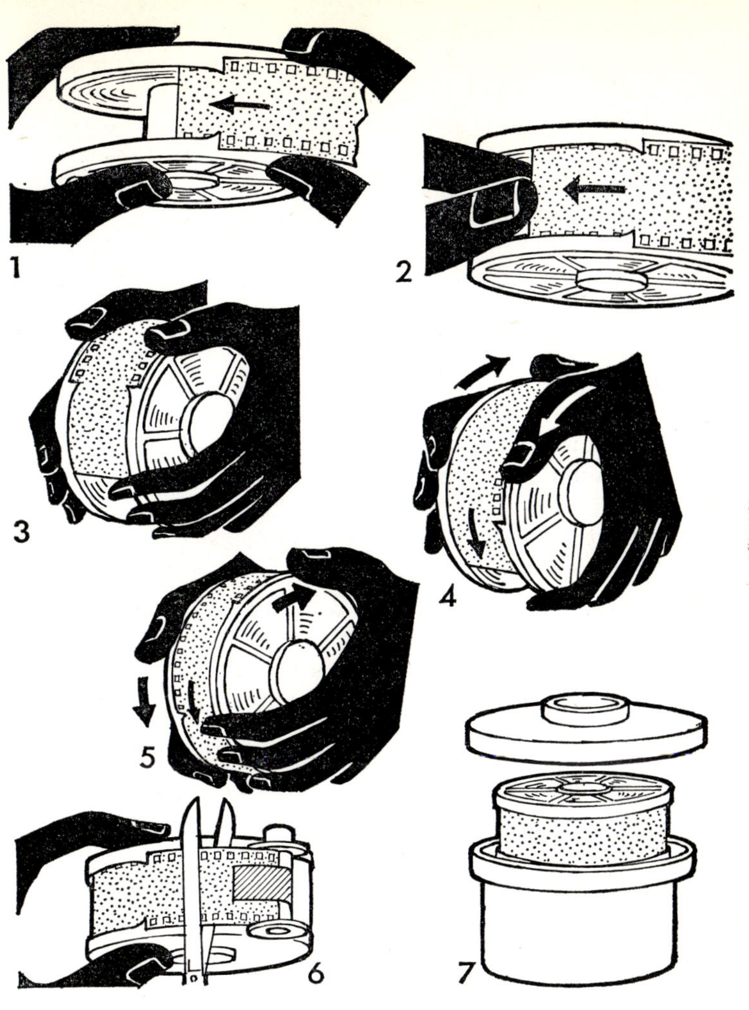

Loading a self-loading spiral. 1, Turn the flanges to line up the openings and gently push the end of the film in. 2, Pull the film farther into the spiral 3, Grip the flanges. 4,5, Rotate and counter rotate the flanges and the film feeds in automatically. 6, Cut or tear the film end from the spool. 7, Place spiral in tank and close with lid.

The procedure for *self-loading spirals* is as follows:

1 Make sure that the openings on both flanges of the spiral are opposite one another and insert the film into the grooves with its emulsion side towards the centre of the spiral.
2 To aid the introduction of the film into the spiral, grip the end of the film and pull it into the spiral for several inches, to ensure that it is brought past the one-way gripping device.
3 Hold the spiral with both hands, so that one thumb is near each groove entrance.
4 Place one thumb on the edge of the film and rotate the flanges against one another. The pressure of your thumb on the film will stop the film coming out of the spiral.
5 Reverse the procedure by applying pressure with your other thumb and rotate the flanges in opposite directions. Repeating the oscillating movement of the flanges causes the film to be drawn into the grooves.
6 When the film is fully loaded, cut or tear the film from the backing paper or film spool. Don't tear the film and tape apart too quickly. This can cause a visible discharge of static electricity which could fog the film.
7 Place the spiral in the tank and put the lid on firmly.

Some people prefer the centre-loading type of spiral in which the film is loaded from the centre outward after clipping the film to the central core. Because 35 mm films are narrower than other roll films, they are easier to use in these spirals, although, with practice, the wider roll films can also be conveniently loaded. The procedure for *centre-loading spirals* is as follows:

1 While holding the spiral in one hand, curve the film by pressing the edges toward one another with the thumb and index finger of your other hand. The film will just clear the grooves.
2 Insert the curved film in the spiral and fasten it to the clip on the central core.
3 Rotate the spiral while gently feeding in the curved film. As the film moves across the grooves and the pressure which holds it curved is released, it drops into the correct groove. Do not allow a groove to be missed or the film

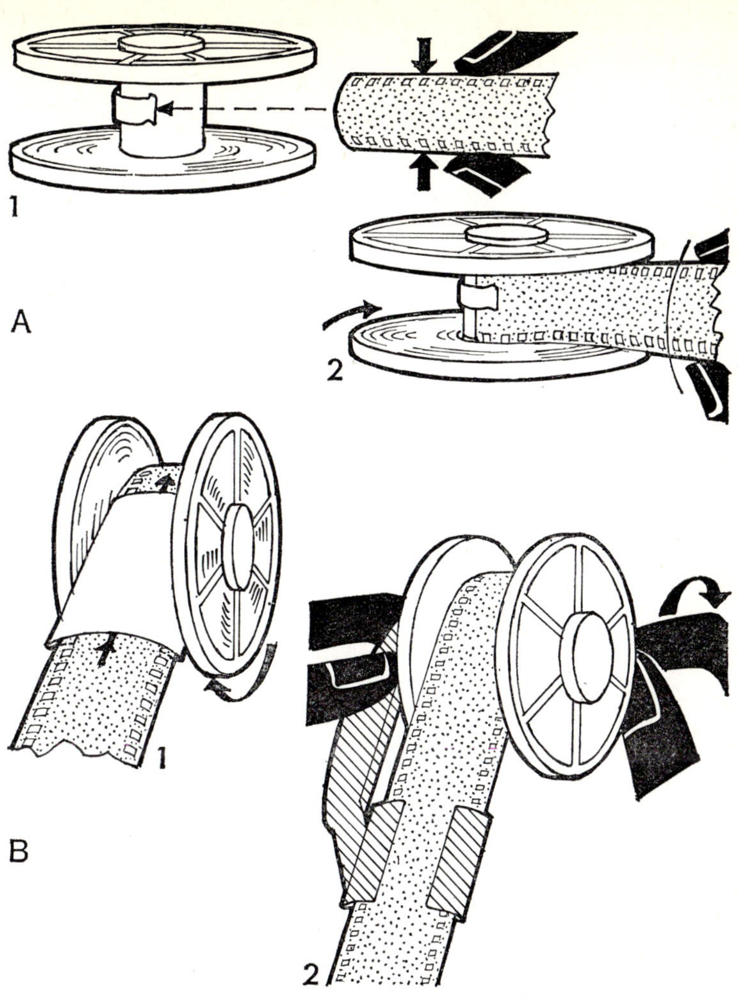

Loading centre-loading and automatic spirals. **A1**, Curve the film gently and push the end into the spiral. 2, Fix the film end under the clip and rotate the spiral while feeding the film in. **B**1,2, Devices for maintaining the curve in the film as it is fed into the spiral.

may buckle and stick to the neighbouring turn, resulting in uneven circulation of processing solutions.

4 Cut the film from the spool or backing paper and place in the developing tank, as shown on page 59.

Automatic-loading spirals are similar to centre-loading spirals, except that they have a loading device to hold the film clear of the grooves when inserting the film in the spiral. The loading procedure is essentially the same as for centre-loading spirals, but the loading device is removed after loading.

Daylight-loading tanks are more varied in the way in which they are loaded because each make of tank is somewhat different in its mode of construction, whereas darkroom-loading tanks have definite spiral types which are loaded in one way regardless of the make of tank.

You should refer to the particular instructions for your make of daylight-loading tank for precise details of the loading operation.

Once you have mastered the loading of the spiral with dummy film in daylight, try repeating the operation in the dark, and practise until you can do it without difficulty. In particular, you should master the following techniques which are required to be carried out in the dark when you use an exposed film.

1 To open the film spool, cassette or cartridge and find the end of the film without getting finger marks on the emulsion.
2 To insert the film in the spiral.
3 To cut or tear the film from the backing paper or spool.
4 To insert the loaded spiral in the tank.
5 To place the lid securely on the tank.

When you are certain that you can carry out these operations successfully in total darkness, you will be ready to process films that have been exposed in your camera.

Processing of Black-and-White Negative Films

A developer solution contains a number of chemicals which are present in appropriate quantities to produce the required photographic result. The choice and 'balancing' of the constituents is done by the manufacturer and results from a great deal of experiment and experience in varying the *composition* of the developer.

The following brief outline of the nature and function of the various developer constituents will help you to understand more about what happens during development.

Developer constituents and their functions

A developer consists of many different chemicals, mainly:

1 The developing agent (or agents).
2 The preservative.
3 The alkali or accelerator.
4 The restrainer.
5 A solvent for the above chemicals.

In addition to these chemicals, developers frequently contain a water-softening agent to avoid difficulties when hard tap water is used.

Developing agents belong to the class of chemical compounds known as reducing agents. Their function is to convert (or reduce) only the exposed silver halide grains of the emulsion to metallic silver, while leaving the unexposed grains unaffected. In doing so, they become oxidised generally to brown-coloured compounds. Their activity in reducing silver halide to metallic silver is controlled to a large extent by the nature and concentration of the alkali. Their ability to discriminate between exposed and unexposed grains is enhanced by the inclusion of a restrainer (to diminish fog formation).

A preservative is also included in developer formulations for two main purposes: to prevent undue oxidation of the developer by oxygen of the air (aerial oxidation) and to react with the oxidised developer and so prevent staining of the negatives by the coloured oxidation products of the developing agents.

Water is used exclusively as the solvent for dissolving the developer constituents. Distilled water is best, but its cost in comparison with tap water does not generally justify its use. The salts present in tap water do not normally give rise to adverse photographic effects, but may cause a precipitate to be formed in the developer. To avoid this, water-softening agents are normally included in developer formulae.

Examples of typical chemicals and their functions in developer solutions are shown in the table.

DEVELOPER INGREDIENTS

Function	Examples of typical chemicals
Developing agent	Hydroquinone, metol, Phenidone
Preservative	Sodium sulphite, potassium metabisulphite.
Alkali	Sodium carbonate, borax.
Restrainer	Potassium bromide, organic antifoggants.

Types of developer

According to the developer formulation, different types of developer may be obtained. Examples of these are:

Normal MQ and PQ developers contain a mixture of metol and hydroquinone or Phenidone and hydroquinone as the developing agents in conjunction with sodium sulphite preservative, sodium carbonate as the accelerator and potassium bromide or organic antifoggant as the restrainer. They give normal contrast and are good general-purpose developers, but have been largely replaced by fine-grain developers.

Fine-grain developers are very widely used and generally contain metol and hydroquinone as the developing agents, although other developing agents may be used. They are slightly less alkaline (active) than normal developers and generally contain borax as the accelerator, together with a relatively high concentration of sodium sulphite preservative, and potassium bromide as the restrainer. These developers are soft working and result in less grain clumping than occurs in normal developers. They yield fine-grain images of low contrast. Fine-grain developers are specially suitable for 35 mm negatives which require considerable enlargement. In developed photographic emulsions the individual grains are not visible. Unless precautions are taken in development, the grains may clump together to form large aggregates which then become apparent on enlargement, giving a grainy appearance to the print. Accordingly, fine-grain developers have been formulated to minimise the clumping or aggregation of grains during development so that the graininess in the enlargement is no longer objectionable.

High-acutance developers give rise to good definition of the fine detail of the image, and some people prefer the results obtained with these developers to those obtained with the more conventional fine-grain developers. High-acutance developers are of low concentration and for their action depends on local exhaustion of the developer in high-density areas next to low-density areas and so enhance the edge contrast.

High-acutance developers can be obtained by diluting a conventional fine-grain developer and increasing the developing time by the recommended amount. Manufacturers of developers will give this information in the instruction sheet accompanying the developer, if appropriate to their formulation. Alternatively, specially formulated high-acutance developers can be bought and used.

High-acutance developers can be used only once, as they are dilute solutions and become exhausted very rapidly.

There are many other types of developer which have been formulated to achieve special results, but these need not concern us here. Differences in developer formulations, resulting in different types of developer, are due to both the selection of the developer constituents and their relative concentrations.

Choosing a developer

Rather than lay down any rigid rules for selection of a particular class of developer with a particular type of film, the best advice is for you initially to follow the film manufacturer's recommendations as to the developer to be used with the film. These recommendations are normally given in the leaflet accompanying the film. If, for any reason, you are not satisfied with the results, then carry out practical tests with other developer formulations until you find one with which you are perfectly satisfied. Most manufacturers recommend a fine-grain or a high-acutance developer for conventional negative films.

Factors influencing development

The main factors affecting development are dilution, agitation, time and temperature. Appropriate conditions for all these variables are specified by the developer manufacturer and should be strictly adhered to.

For a given developer dilution, the contrast, maximum density and fog level of the negative increase with increases in agitation, time and temperature. To obtain films that are uniformly developed, all these conditions must be controlled.

Effect of dilution

Dilution of developers is specified by the manufacturer and it is ill-advised to depart from these recommendations because the dilution factors have been optimised for the particular film-developer combination. Dilution of a developer beyond the specified dilution not only alters the rate of development, but also may cause unwanted development effects to occur, similar to those given below under agitation.

If the developer is diluted and the time of development increased to compensate for the dilution, results identical with those obtained when using the recommended dilution and development time may not be obtained.

Effect of agitation

It is important to agitate the film in the tank properly during development to avoid uneven development and various unwanted development effects. For example, if no agitation at all is carried out, the areas close to the highlights become occupied with exhausted developer, which causes development to be inhibited in these areas. The *shadow* areas, however, are almost unaffected, because there is little density in these areas and hence little exhausted developer is present. The net result is a reduction in contrast of the negative.

These effects are particularly important with modern spiral tanks in which the film is coiled quite closely. Agitation is normally carried out either by inverting the tank intermittently during the time of development (inversion agitation) or by rotating the spiral with an external stirrer which slots into the spiral core.

Most modern tanks are provided with a plastic cap which fits over the opening for pouring solutions into the tank. With the cap in place, the tank is watertight and can be turned upside down. Sufficient space is provided in the tank above the normal solution level so that when the tank is inverted the developer flows across the film coils.

For efficient agitation, invert the tank for about 10 seconds (four inversions) at one-minute intervals throughout development, unless instructed otherwise.

To give you some idea of the influence of agitation on the rate of development, development times are about 25–50 per cent longer when intermittent agitation is used than for continuous agitation.

Effect of development time

The time of development has a marked influence on the negatives. Over-development leads to increase in density and contrast, while under-development leads to low contrast and density. Accordingly, your film must be developed for the recommended time at the recommended temperature. It is these two variables that require the strictest possible control, assuming that a standardised agitation procedure is used. When timing development, bear in mind that it takes a finite time to drain developer from the tank, during which development is continuing, so start pouring developer from the tank 10 seconds before the specified end of development. Then you can be sure that the tank is empty and drained at the end of the stated

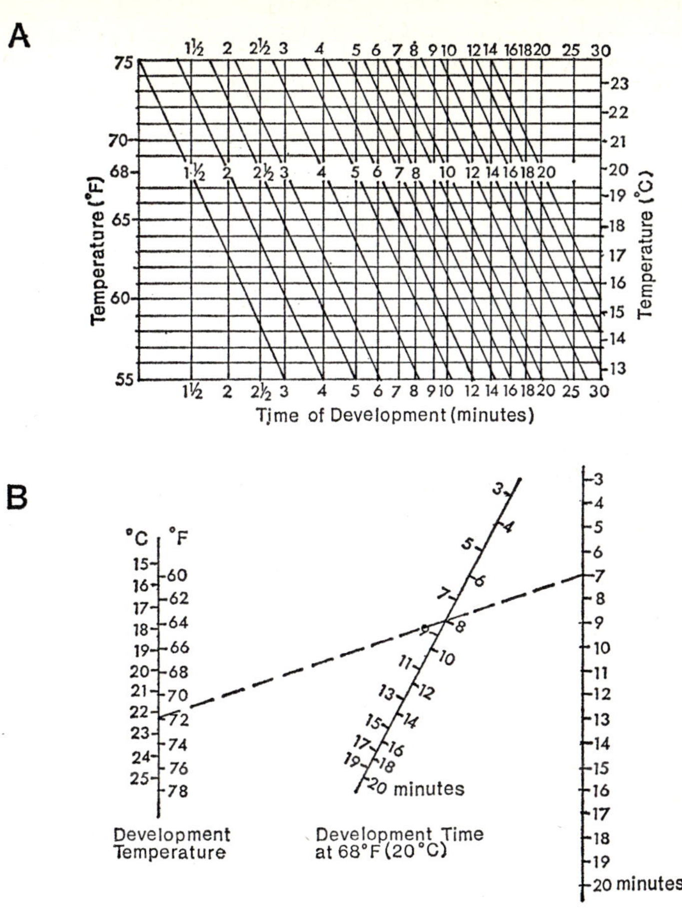

Time-temperature charts. **A,** Typical chart (Ilford Ltd) showing development times at various solution temperatures. **B** Nomograph (May & Baker Ltd) serving the same purpose. See page 70 for instructions.

development time, following which the next stage of processing can be carried out.

Effect of developer temperature

Increase in development temperature can lead to over-development and a decrease in temperature from the manufacturer's recommendations can lead to under-development, similar to the effects produced by changes in development time from that recommended.

The standard development temperature normally quoted is 68°F or 20°C and development times are given for this temperature. Time and temperature are interrelated, and if for any reason it is not possible to obtain a temperature of 68°F or 20°C it is possible to alter the development time to achieve an identical result. For this purpose, most manufacturers publish simplified charts from which it is possible to read the appropriate development time at temperatures other than 68°F or 20°C. A typical chart is shown on page 69. (A)

In order to use this chart, the diagonal line from the recommended time at 68°F or 20°C is followed until it cuts the horizontal line representing the actual temperature to be used. The development time is then read from the bottom line vertically below the intersection. In order to use the time-temperature development chart, just find the recommended development at the published temperature, which is usually 68°F or 20°C. Then follow the diagonal line corresponding to this time until it cuts across a horizontal line representing the development temperature which is going to be used. The time vertically below this intersection represents the required development time.

Thus, if the quoted development time is four minutes at 68°F or 20°C, at 73°F or 23°C the required development time is three minutes.

Alternatively, manufacturers may publish a nomograph for development times at various temperatures. A typical nomograph is shown on page 69. (B)

In order to use the nomograph, the actual development temperature is located on the scale A and the recommended

development time at 68°F or 20°C is located on scale B. A straight line joining these points A and B is extended to scale C, which gives the development time at the temperature selected. Thus, if the development time was eight minutes at 68°F (20°C), at 72°F the required development time is seven minutes.
It is extremely important to maintain the temperature at a constant value throughout the time of development. For development of black-and-white materials, variations of ± 1°F or $\pm \frac{1}{2}$°C are allowable. If the room temperature is very much different from the development temperature, some difficulty may be experienced in keeping the development temperature within these limits. A simple way to keep the development temperature constant is to stand the tank in a bowl of water at the development temperature. If the temperature varies, it can be controlled by the addition of hot or cold water to the water bath. Before processing, all bottles of solutions to be used should be stood in a water bath at the temperature of processing until they have reached the working temperature.
The easiest way of keeping the development temperature constant is to make sure that the development temperature and the ambient temperature are the same, but this may not always be possible.

Working life of developer solution

It is generally recommended that a fresh developer solution is used for developing each film (one-shot processing). This is a very convenient procedure, especially when using concentrated liquid developers or developer stock solutions prepared from powdered chemicals. Exhaustion of developers is then not a problem, because fresh developer is used each time.
As the developer is used it suffers a gradual loss in activity by oxidation of the developing agents and the release of soluble bromides (restrainers) from the film which is being developed. Also, during the development reaction the alkalinity of the developer decreases, which reduces the developer activity. Some developers may be used for processing more than one

film by increasing the development by a certain time for each successive film, to compensate for the loss in developer activity This is somewhat more economical than the one-shot method, in which the developer is discarded after use. There is, however, a limit to doing this, when increasing the time of development cannot compensate for the exhaustion of the developer. Typical recommendations might be a 10 per cent increase in time for each successive film up to a maximum number of ten films.

Alternatively, *replenishers* may be used. These are solutions of special composition which, when added to a used developer, bring its activity back to its original working activity. This involves the preparation of an extra replenisher solution and is only warranted when a reasonably large number of films are going to be developed.

For the home-processor the one-shot system is the most convenient because he is assured of consistent developer activity, provided that the stock solution is correctly stored. Also, no additional solutions need be prepared.

Developing the film

So far, the composition, function and variables of developers have been considered, but few details of the practice of development have been given.

Once the tank has been loaded (page 56) and the developer been prepared (page 46), proceed as follows:

1 Pour the developer (at the correct temperature) into the tank and start the timer or note the time on your clock or watch.
2 Gently but firmly tap the bottom of the tank on a table to dislodge any air bubbles that may have stuck to the film surface.
3 Lift the tank from the table and slowly turn upside down. Repeat this inversion agitation (page 68) for about 30 seconds or eight inversions at the start of development.
4 Check the temperature of the developer and place the tank in a bowl of warm or cold water, if necessary, to bring the temperature to that specified (see page 71).

5 Carry out inversion agitation for about 10 seconds at four inversions every minute.
6 Ten seconds before the end of the specified time, pour the developer from the tank and drain thoroughly.

Development is now completed and a rinse or stop bath is then used prior to fixation.

Stopping the developing action

Residual developer remaining in the film after draining the tank will cause continuation of development. An intermediate rinse is given before fixation to remove as much as possible of the developer remaining in the film. However, even this does not stop development, but only slows it down. Development may be stopped completely by an acidic stop bath such as 1 per cent acetic acid prior to fixation, although with modern acid or acid-hardening fixers (see page 76) an intermediate rinse suffices. This is carried out by pouring in water and continuously agitating by inversion for about 30 seconds to one minute and then pouring away.

Constituents of fixing solutions

We saw earlier (page 11) that the purpose of fixation is to remove unexposed silver halides from the emulsion. To do this the main ingredient of a fixing bath is a solvent for silver halides. During fixation, soluble silver thiosulphate complexes are formed which diffuse from the film into the solution. Any residual soluble complexes remaining in the film are then completely removed by washing (see page 78).

The most commonly used silver halide solvent is sodium thiosulphate pentahydrate, which is popularly known as '*hypo*'. A satisfactory fixing bath can be prepared by making up a 20 per cent solution of hypo, but this plain or neutral fixer has certain disadvantages if it is used for fixing films which have been rinsed in water after development. Staining of the nega-

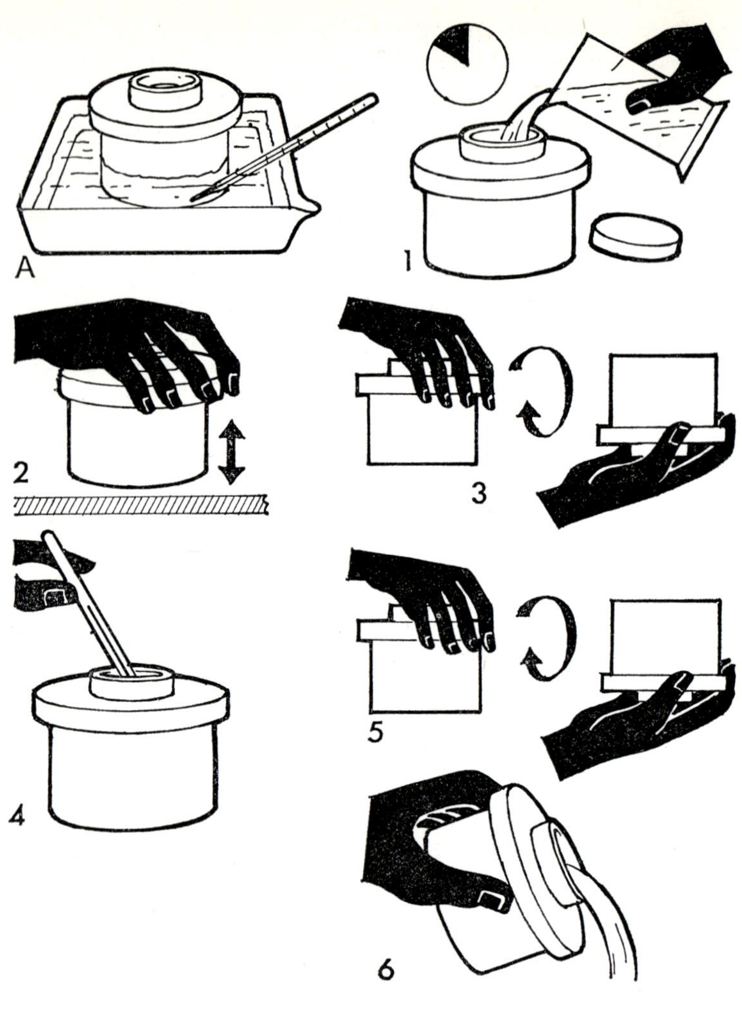

Developing the film. A, Waterbath to maintain solution temperature during processing. 1, Pour developer into tank at recommended temperature and start timer. 2, Tap tank gently on bench to dislodge air bubbles. 3, Agitate for about 30 seconds. 4, Check temperature. 5, Agitate for 10 seconds every minute. 6, At the end of development time, empty tank.

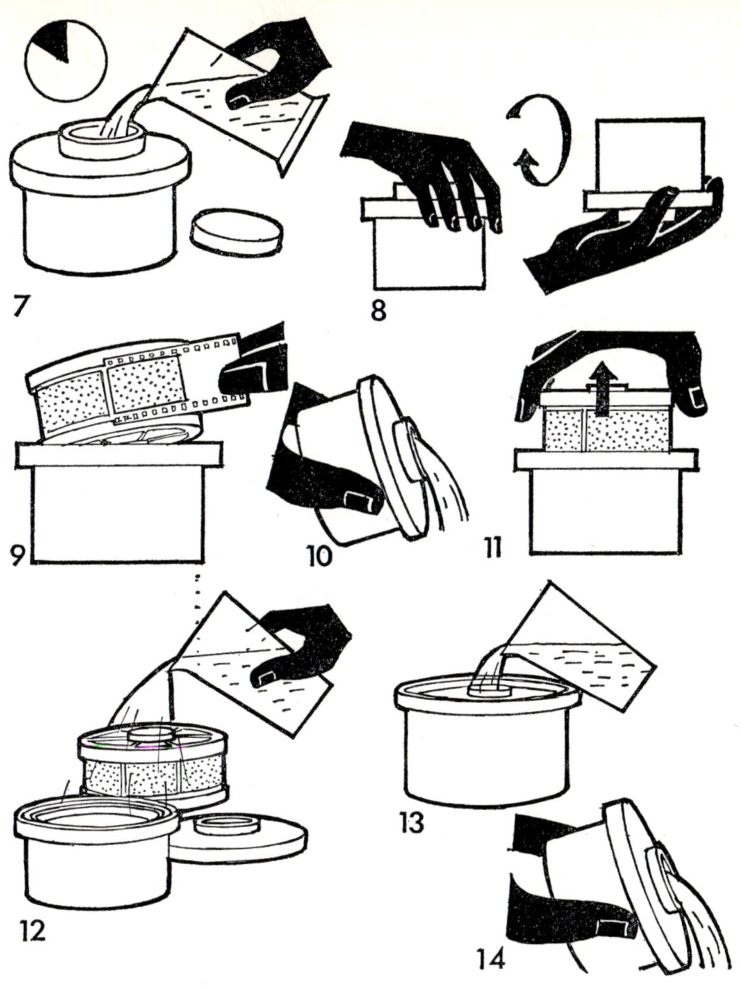

Fixing and washing in changes of water. 7, Pour in fixer at correct temperature. A rinse or stop bath can be used before this step. 8, Agitate for 30 seconds initially and then for 5 seconds every minute. 9, Inspect film at end of fixing time. 10, If clear, pour out fixer. 11, Remove spiral from tank. 12, Rinse tank spiral and lid. 13, Replace spiral and fill tank with water. 14, Pour out water and refill tank 5-8 times at five minute intervals. Add wetting agent to final wash before drying.

tives may result, owing to carry over of developer into the fixer. If a plain or neutral fixer is used, an acid stop bath must always be used after development.

Alternatively, acid fixers have been formulated which avoid the need for an intermediate stop bath and also avoid staining. Acid-fixing baths contain hypo and a weak acid such as acetic acid in conjunction with sodium sulphite. The final ingredient which is frequently used is a hardening agent, which raises the melting temperature of the emulsion and reduces its amount of swelling. This means that films are less likely to be damaged when processing at high temperatures (see page 148), and also the drying time is reduced because the emulsion layer is not swollen very much and therefore takes up less water.

Acid-hardening fixing baths should be used whenever possible because they combine the desirable properties of all types of fixing baths and are the least likely to cause trouble. A summary of the ingredients of fixing baths is given in the table.

FIXING BATH INGREDIENTS

Function	Examples of typical chemicals
Fixing agent	Sodium thiosulphate pentahydrate (hypo), ammonium thiosulphate*.
Acid	Potassium metabisulphite, acetic acid/sodium sulphite.
Hardening agent	Potash alum, chrome alum.

*Used in rapid fixing baths (see page 142).

Completion of fixation

Fixation is complete when all the unexposed silver halides have formed a soluble complex with sodium thiosulphate. However, this process cannot be seen to have gone to completion and, as a general rule, a film is considered fixed when it has remained in the fixing bath for twice the clearing time: generally, 10–20 minutes is an adequate time for fixation. If, after approximately five minutes' fixation, the film is still cloudy, replace it in the fixer until it is perfectly clear.

The rate of fixation depends upon a number of factors: the

type and thickness of the emulsion, temperature, agitation, amount of exposure, the type and composition of the fixing bath, and its degree of exhaustion. Specified fixing times normally have a wide safety margin to take these factors into account. Fixation is a far less critical process than development, and factors such as time, temperature and agitation do not have to be controlled to the same degree of precision that is essential for development.

Fixer exhaustion

Thorough fixation is essential if negatives are to be kept for any length of time. Failure to fix negatives properly will result in staining, and even fading, of negatives. Exhaustion of fixing baths with use is caused by a number of factors, the main ones being:

1 Dilution of the fixing bath, because some water is carried over on each film from the rinse bath while a small quantity of the fixer is removed with the film at the end of fixation.
2 Carry-over of alkaline developer causes the fixer to become less acidic, which results in a greater propensity for staining and may cause a decrease in hardening efficiency.
3 The concentration of hypo is reduced because it combines with the silver halide to form a soluble silver thiosulphate compound.
4 Accompanying 3 there is build-up in the silver concentration in the fixer solution.
5 Exhaustion of the fixing bath by the cumulative effects of the above factors after a number of films have been fixed.

The net result of all these factors is that the fixing becomes less and less efficient as the bath is used and the clearing time is increased.

As a general guideline, a fixing bath is discarded when the clearing time is twice as long as that for the fresh fixer. For the home-processor who buys proprietary fixers, the maximum number of films which can be properly fixed in a given volume of fixing bath will almost certainly be stated by the supplier.

Fixing the film

Although the temperature of fixation is not very critical, it is best to fix films at or around the development temperature (development temperature $\pm$3°F or $\pm$2°C) to avoid subjecting the film to sudden temperature changes, which may cause reticulation (see page 185). The procedure is as follows:

1 After the tank has been drained of rinse water or stop bath, pour in fixer at the appropriate temperature and set the timer or note the time on your clock or watch.
2 Agitate continuously for about the first 30 seconds (10–12 inversions) and for about five seconds (or two inversions) every minute.
3 Continue fixing for 10 minutes or other recommended time. Then remove the lid, lift out the spiral, and inspect the film for cloudiness.
4 If clear, pour out fixer and drain tank. If not clear, continue fixing until clear then pour out fixer.

Washing the film

If permanent stable images are required, efficient washing is essential. The purpose of washing is to remove all the soluble salts from the film. The main ones are soluble silver complexes and hypo. If soluble silver complexes are allowed to remain in the film, they can in time decompose to form a yellow-brown stain. Residual hypo can cause fading of the silver image and staining. The importance of efficient washing should, therefore, never be underestimated.

There are two main methods of washing films: these are washing in changes of water and washing in running water. If possible, avoid washing in water that has a temperature vastly different from that of the developer and fixer. Negatives can be ruined by going from a fixer at 68°F or 20°C to water at 50°F or 10°C or even less. A sudden reduction or increase in the temperature of the emulsions can cause a rapid contraction or expansion of the emulsion, resulting in a mosaic-like pattern on the surface of the film (reticulation).

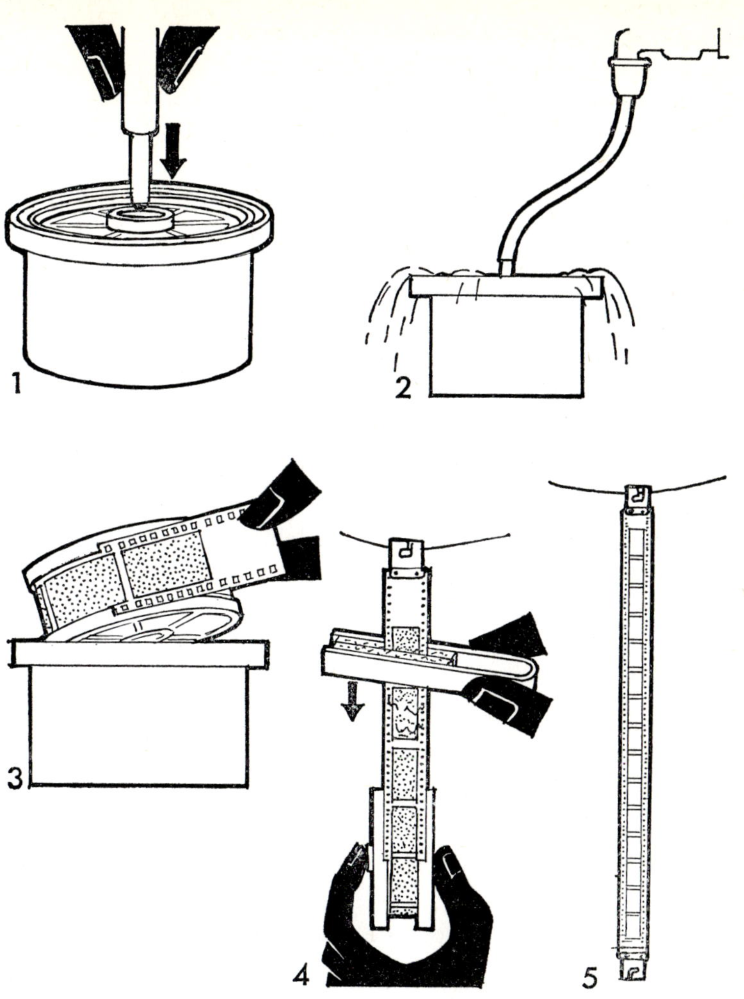

Washing and drying. 1, After fixing, remove tank lid and push thin hose attached to cold water tap into centre of spiral. 2, Run water for 30 minutes. 3, Add wetting agent to final one-minute soak. 4, Remove film from spiral and hang up to dry. Droplets may be wiped off at this stage. 5, Leave film in dust-free atmosphere until dry.

After washing, the film is given a final rinse in a photographic-grade wetting agent to ensure even draining of water from the film and to avoid drying marks.

Washing in changes of water

This procedure can be used when no running water is available or when water supplies are restricted. It is a more efficient and economical procedure than washing in running water, although it requires more work (see page 75).

1 After fixing is complete, remove the spiral from the tank.
2 Rinse the tank, spiral and lid with water.
3 Replace the spiral in the tank and fill with water. Agitate for a few seconds and leave for five minutes.
4 After five minutes, agitate again and thoroughly drain the tank and spiral
5 Refill the tank and repeat procedures 3 and 4 a further 5–8 times.
6 Add a few drops of a photographic-grade wetting agent to the final rinse.

Washing in running water

This is the simplest method and may be carried out as follows:

1 Remove the lid from the tank and push the end of a short length of hose attached to the cold water tap into the centre core of the spiral. (see page 79)
2 Turn on the tap and wash for 30 minutes with a moderate flow of water.
3 After 30 minutes, turn off the tap and add a few drops of a photographic-grade wetting agent to the water in the tank, agitate the spiral for a few seconds and leave for approximately one minute.

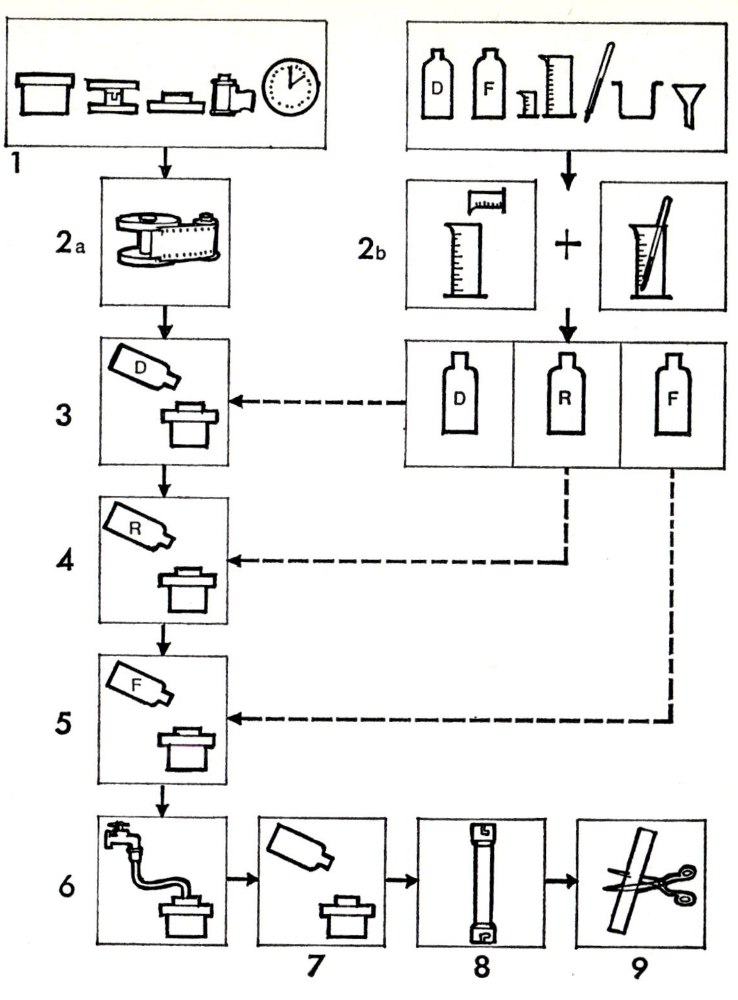

Processing stages for black and white negatives. 1, Arrange equipment in logical sequence. 2a, Load tank. 2b, Prepare solutions. 3, Develop. 4, Rinse or stop bath. 5, Fix. 6, Wash. 7, Add wetting agent. 8, Dry. 9, Cut film into suitable lengths for storage.

Drying the film

It is best to hang your films in a draught-free and dust-free place until they are dry. A convenient place would be a spare bedroom, if available. Always use a weighted clip attached to the lower end of the film, to prevent the film from curling. Before leaving the film to dry, both sides of the film should be wiped with a viscous sponge or film wiper to remove superfluous water and so encourage even and more rapid drying.
Drying can be accelerated by using an electric fan heater, but make sure that the temperature does not exceed about 86°F or 30°C otherwise melting of the emulsion layer may occur. Also, do not allow water to drip from the film on to the heater.

1 After the final rinse, take out the spiral and place across the top of the tank. Attach a clip to the end of the film.
2 Hang the film by the clip in a convenient place not too close to a wall and unwind the film from the spiral. While unwinding, draw a moistened film wiper down the length of the film.
3 Attach a weighted clip to the bottom of the film and leave to dry.

The processing of your film is now complete, but do not ruin all your careful work by rolling up the film and putting it in a drawer. Films are best stored in negative wallets or albums, after cutting into appropriate lengths. This will keep your film free from scratches.

Summary of procedure

1 Get all the equipment that you need ready and lay it out in a logical sequence.
2a Load the tank (see page 56).
2b Prepare the working strength solutions that you are going to use and make sure that they are at the correct temperature (see page 46).
3 Pour the developer into the tank to start development (see page 72).

4 After pouring out the developer, pour in the rinse or stop bath (see page 73).
5 Pour out the rinse or stop bath and add the fixer (see page 78).
6 When fixation is complete, pour out the fixer and thoroughly wash the film (see page 80).
7 Add wetting agent to the wash water (see page 80).
8 Hang the film up to dry (see page 82).
9 When the film is dry, cut it into short lengths and store it in negative bags.

Processing Colour Negative Films

At the time of writing home-processing kits suitable for the small scale amateur user are provided by both Kodak and Agfa. Also there are many such processing kits offered by independent manufacturers. These chemicals are in the form of liquid concentrates or powdered chemicals (see page 46). Usually the solutions are discarded immediately after use and the shelf-life of the working strength solutions are limited to about 6 weeks for colour developers and up to about 12 weeks for the other solutions.

Almost all currently available colour negative films fall into two basic types according to the processing chemistry that *must* be used. Firstly there are those of the Kodak type that must be processed in Kodak C-41 (Flexicolor) chemicals or their equivalents. These films include: Cilcolor, Fujicolor F-II and F-II 400, Kodacolor II and 400, Kranzcolor, 3M Color Print, Ogacolor, Sakuracolor II and 400, and Turacolor II.

Secondly there is a smaller group of films that must be processed in Agfacolor chemicals or their equivalents. These include: Agfacolor CNS 2, Agfacolor 80 S, Orwocolor, Perucolor and Technicolor Print.

Comparison with black-and-white processing

The processing of colour negative materials is only slightly different from the processing of black-and-white negative materials. In colour negative processing, dye images are formed together with unwanted silver images in the development stage. The unwanted silver image is removed after development in two stages: first, a *bleach* solution is used to convert the silver into silver bromide; and, secondly, the silver bromide, together with the unexposed silver halides, is removed in a conventional fixing bath.

More solutions are required for colour negative processing, more steps are used and the control of colour negative processing is far more critical. Colour films are more susceptible to temperature variations and to mechanical damage. In general, more care is required for their processing and the manufacturer's recommendations must be followed meticulously. For example, slight over-development of a black-and-white negative will yield a negative that can give a perfectly acceptable print, whereas with a colour negative over-development will almost certainly yield a negative that will not give a satisfactory print. In colour processing, three emulsions are developed to form three dyes (see page 19) and any variation in processing is likely to affect the different layers by different amounts, resulting in a negative that is 'out of colour balance', for which adjustments cannot be made when it is printed.

Equipment for processing

No special or additional equipment is required for processing colour negative films other than more bottles to store the extra solutions and an accurate thermometer to ensure that variations in processing temperatures are kept within the specified limits. The basic equipment recommended for black-and-white negative processing (see page 35) is perfectly suitable for processing colour negatives. A water bath in which to stand the bottles of solutions and the developing tank during processing will be needed to maintain the temperature (see page 71).

Colour developer constituents

The solution used for colour development is very similar to that used for black-and-white development (see page 64), although its composition is somewhat different.

In colour development it is the developer oxidation product that is required to form the image and not the silver. When the developing agent converts the exposed silver halide grains to metallic silver, it becomes oxidized and it is this oxidation product of the developing agent that combines with *colour formers* (or *colour couplers*) present in the emulsion layers (see page 195) to form dyes. Accordingly, colour developers employ special developing agents and contain considerably less sodium sulphite preservative than black-and-white developers because sodium sulphite also combines with the oxidised developing agent (see page 64). The other ingredients such as the alkali and restrainer are essentially similar to those used in black- and-white developers.

Control of colour development

Unlike black-and-white development, colour development is always carried out at fixed temperature for a given time. Time-temperature charts (see page 70) are never applied to colour development. The temperature must be maintained within $\frac{1}{2}$°F or $\frac{1}{4}$°C for most colour processes, whereas temperatures for black-and-white development need only be maintained to within ± 1°F or $\frac{1}{2}$°C. This means that a water bath surrounding the developing tank is likely to be needed (see page 71). On very hot days, ice may have to be added to the water bath to maintain the temperature at the correct value. Remember to check the temperature of the developer at regular intervals throughout the development time and make the appropriate adjustments.

Processes following colour development

A complete summary for the Kodak C-41 and Agfacolor processes is given in tabular form on page 89.

Stop or intermediate bath. Immediately following development, a stop or intermediate bath is used. For the Agfacolor process the intermediate bath also contains colour developer so the time of treatment and the temperature in this bath must be as carefully controlled as the development stage. For the Kodak C-41 process no stop bath is used, the bleach immediately follows development.

First wash. After the stop or intermediate bath, the film is given a thorough wash to remove the bulk of the processing chemicals.

First wash. After the stop or intermediate bath, the film is given a thorough wash to remove the bulk of the processing chemicals.
In the Kodak C-41 process the first wash comes after the bleach.

Bleach. Following the wash, or development a bleach bath is used to convert the silver image to silver bromide. This is the major function of the bleach in the Kodak C-41 process together with the subsidiary function of the destruction of the yellow filter layer, but in the Agfacolor process this bleach bath is very critical as it not only converts the silver to silver bromide and destroys the yellow filter layer but also controls the formation of the colour mask. Bleach baths generally contain potassium ferricyanide or iron sequestrene and potassium bromide as the active constituents.

Second wash. After bleaching the silver image, an intermediate wash is normally carried out.

Fix. The film now contains the dye images together with silver halides, which are now removed by a conventional fixing bath.

Final wash and dry. After fixing, washing and drying are carried out in an analogous manner to that used for black-and-white negative materials (see page 78) but a final rinse in a stabilizing bath is used.

Summary of procedures

The following table summarizes the processing steps of the Kodak C-41 and Agfacolor Processes.

PROCESSING KODAK AND AGFACOLOR COLOUR NEGATIVES

	Agfacolor Process 70 Kodak C-41			Agfacolor N		
Stage	No.	Time (min)	Temp (°C)	No.	Time (min)	Temp (°C)
Colour develop	1	3/15	37·8 ±0·15	1	8	20 ±0·2
Stop or intermediate bath				2	4	20 ±0·5
Wash				3	14	14–20
Bleach	2	6/30	24–41	4	6	20±0·5
Wash	3	3/15	37·8±3	5	6	14–20
Fix	4	6/30	24–41	6	6	20±1
Final wash	5	3/15	37·8±3	7	10	20±1
Stabilizer	6	1/30	24–41			
Dry	7	–	43	8	–	35
Total time (excluding drying)		20 min/20 sec			54 minutes	

After processing your colour negative films, protect them from mechanical damage by storing them in negative wallets. Colour

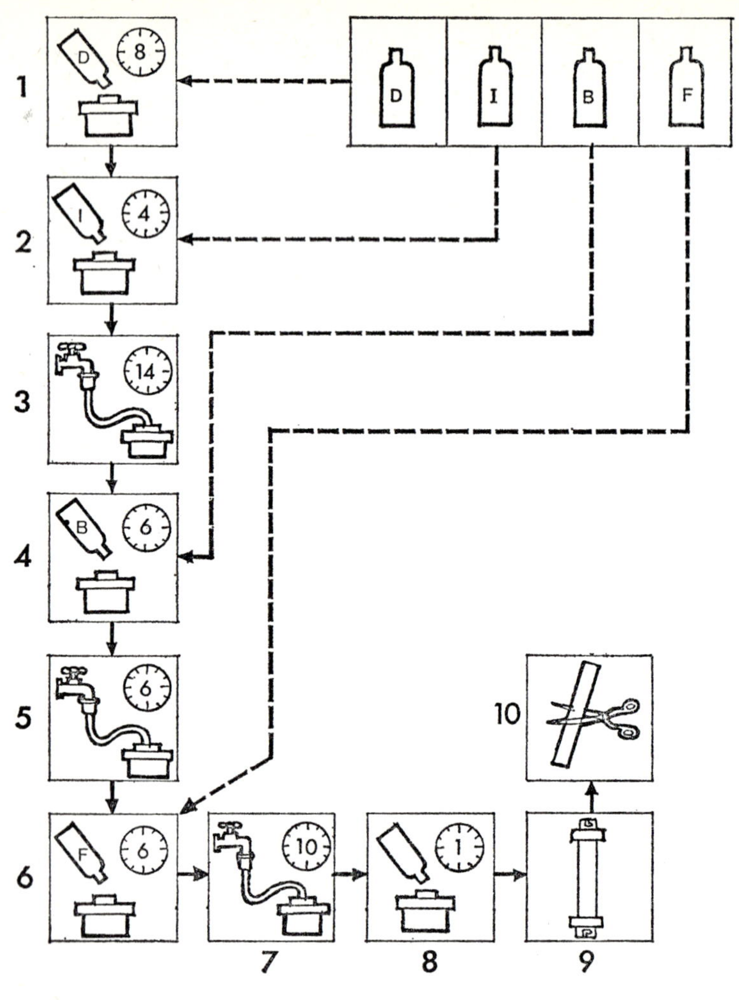

Processing Agfacolor negative films. 1, Develop for 8 minutes at 20°C. 2, Intermediate bath 4 minutes. 3, Wash 14 minutes. 4, Bleach 6 minutes. 5, Wash 6 minutes. 6, Fix 6 minutes. 7, Wash 10 minutes. 8, Rinse plus wetting agent 1 minute. 9, Dry. 10, Store.

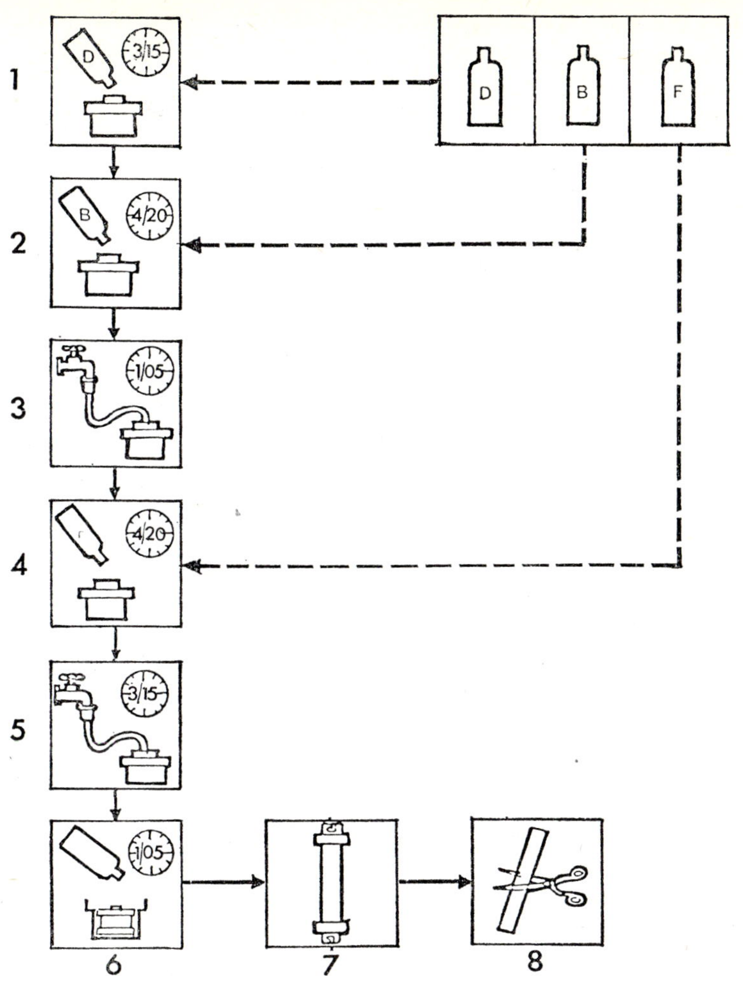

C-41 (Flexicolor) Process for Kodacolor II and similar films. 1, Develop for 3 minutes 15 seconds at 37·8°C. 2, Bleach 4 minutes 20 seconds. 3, Wash 1 minute 05 seconds. 4, Fix 4 minutes 20 seconds. 5, Wash 3 minutes 15 seconds. 6, Stabilize 1 minute 05 seconds. 7, Dry. 8, Store.

films, even when dry, are more susceptible to damage than are black-and-white films.

Constant exposure to daylight, moisture or heat may cause the dyes to fade, so colour negatives are best stored in a place that is dark, cool and dry.

Some independent suppliers of processing chemicals provide concentrated liquid chemicals and have simplified the processing procedure by making use of a single *bleach-fix* solution in place of the separate bleaching and fixing solutions that are normally required. Two examples of this alternative chemistry are Unicolor K2 chemicals (Unicolor Division, Photo Systems Inc., Dexter, Michigan 48130, USA) and Photocolor II chemicals (Photo Technology Ltd., Potters Bar, Hertfordshire, England). Both are used for the simplified processing of Kodacolor II type films (C-41 alternative process). The processing sequences for these chemicals are summarized in the table below.

ALTERNATIVE C-41 PROCESSING

	Unicolor K2			Photocolor II		
Stage	No.	Time (min/sec)	Temp (°C)	No.	Time (min/sec)	Temp (°C)
Colour develop	1	3/15	38	1	2/45	38
Stop bath	–	—	—	2	0/30	38
Bleach-fix	2	6/00	38	3	3/00	38
Wash	3	3/00	38	4	5/00	30–35
Rinse/stabilize	4	0/30	38	5	0/30	30–35
Dry	5	—	43	6	—	43
Total time (excluding drying)		12min 45sec			11min 45sec	

The above summary of colour processing shows that by following a relatively simple procedure it is easy to process colour negative films. Manufacturers' literature should be consulted for more exact details of processing, such as agitation recommendations, and to check on possible alterations or modifications to existing films or processes.

Reversal Processing of Black-and-White Films

Any negative material can be reversal processed, but those intended for this form of processing are normally specially designed. Nevertheless, many film manufacturers publish formulae for the reversal processing of some of their normal black-and-white negative films, and the home-processor should consult such literature or contact his photographic dealer to find out whether his film is suitable for reversal processing and if so whether suitable solutions are available. Universal processing kits are, however, available complete with instructions for the reversal processing of most manufacturer's black-and-white negative films.

Principles of reversal processing

Reversal processing is not a simple process, and the procedure differs for each type of film. Always follow the manufacturer's recommendations and do not be tempted to process one manufacturer's film in another manufacturer's solutions, because results will be disappointing and may result in total failure.

Reversal processing involves more solutions and steps than negative processing and results in the formation of positive images suitable for the preparation of slides or transparencies for viewing in a projector or simple hand viewer.

The function and purpose of the numerous steps involved are given below in a generalised form which is common to nearly all reversal processing procedures.

First development

After exposing the film and loading it in a conventional developing tank, the first or negative development stage is carried out. In this stage, the latent image is developed to form a negative image by means of a specially formulated developer which, in addition to the normal negative developer constituents (see page 64), contains a small quantity of a silver halide solvent, such as hypo. This reduces the densities of the positive image

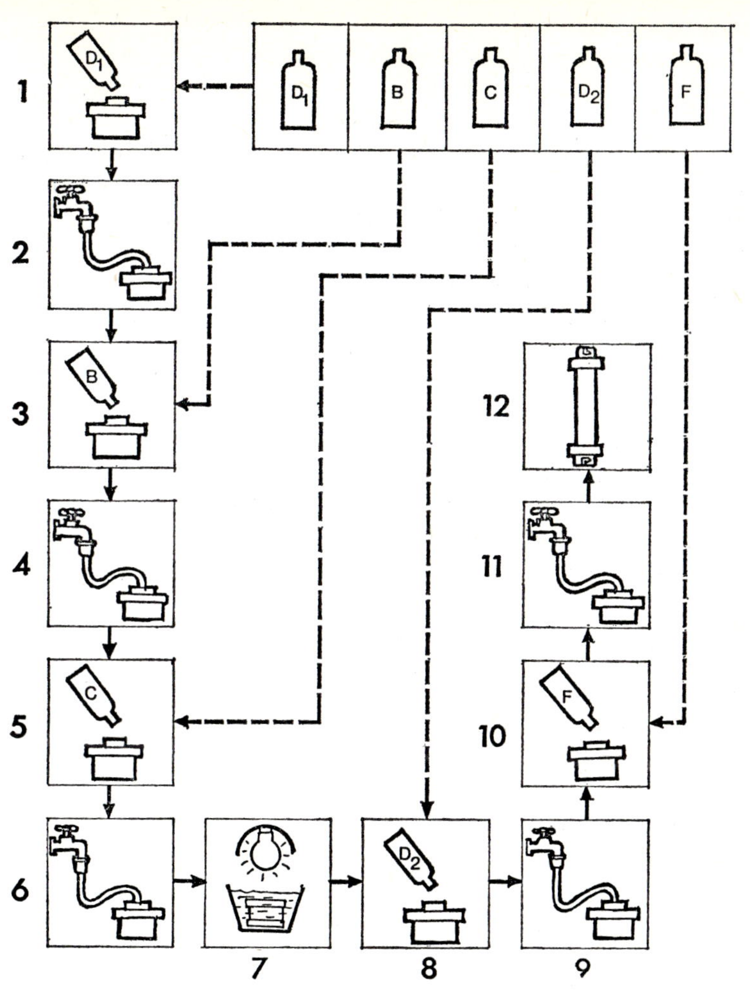

Reversal processing of black and white films. 1, First develop. 2, Wash. 3, Bleach. 4, Wash. 5, Clear. 6, Wash. 7, Re-expose. 8, Second develop. 9, Wash. 10, Fix. 11, Wash. 12, Dry

eventually obtained and increases the exposure *latitude* of the film, because it removes some of the silver halide and so leaves less in the emulsion for second development. Fog is reduced and 'clearer' results are obtained.

First development is the most critical of the processing steps and requires careful control because it affects the quantity of silver halide remaining for subsequent development to a positive image. Over-development at this stage results in a thin transparency, while under-development results in a transparency that is too dense. Time and temperature, therefore, are carefully controlled, as in negative processing.

Wash

Immediately following first development, the film is washed in running water to remove developer chemicals and to stop development.

Bleach

The negative silver image formed during the first development is next dissolved in a bleach while leaving the unexposed grains unaffected. To ensure complete removal of the negative image, agitation must be thorough.

This bleach solution is of a totally different composition to those used in colour processing (see page 89), and normally contains potassium dichromate or permanganate and sulphuric acid. Which oxidise metallic silver to soluble silver sulphate.

Following the bleach bath, the film is washed in running water to remove the bulk of the bleach chemicals.

Clearing

After bleaching the silver image, the film is stained by the products of the reaction between bleach bath constituents and the silver image (brown manganese dioxide from the perman-

Notes: The first nine prints on the following pages were all made on the same grade of paper processed under identical processing conditions, using the same exposure based on integrated light readings through the enlarger lens. These prints do not necessarily represent the best print, other than for the correctly exposed and developed negative, but provide a valid means of comparison of the various negatives. Better prints could be obtained by varying the grade of paper and the exposure used in their printing.

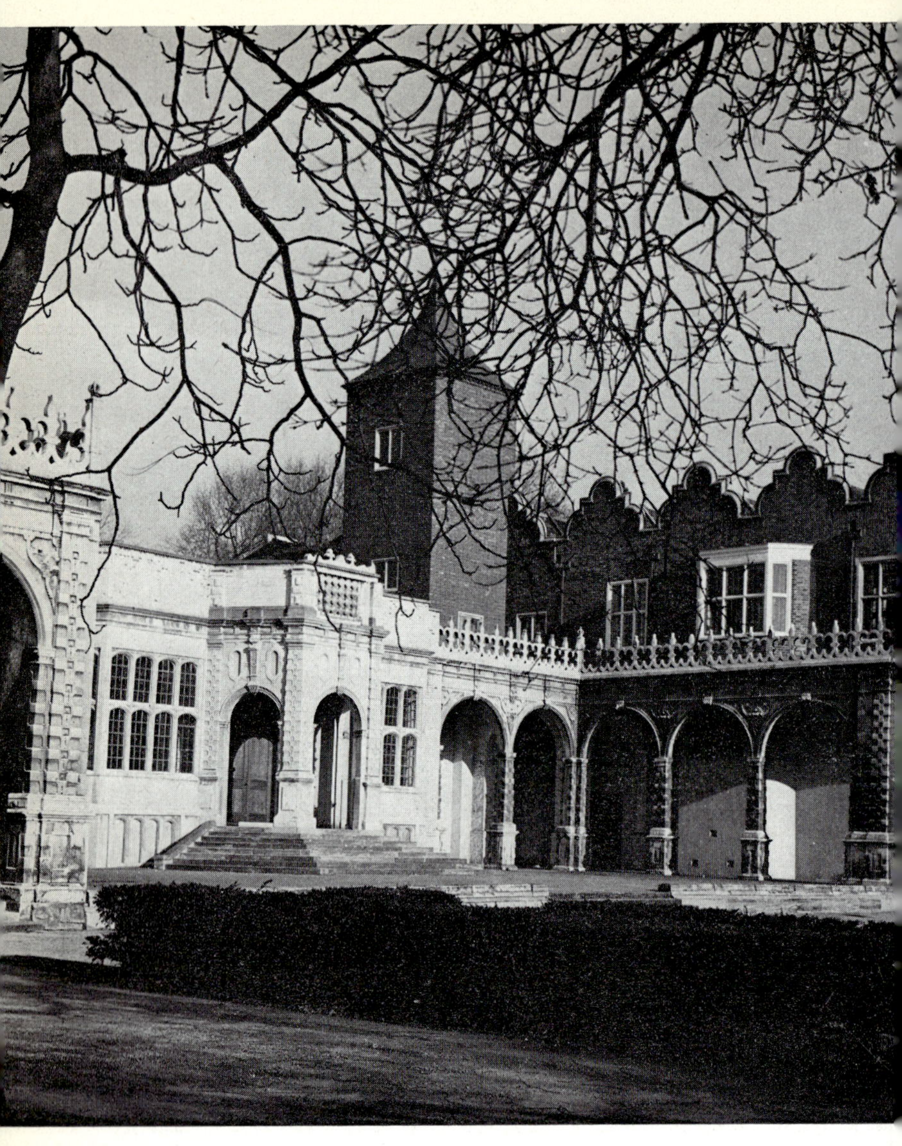

Print from correctly exposed and developed negative (opposite)
In the print detail is apparent in the shadows and the highlights whilst giving a full range of tones between black and white.

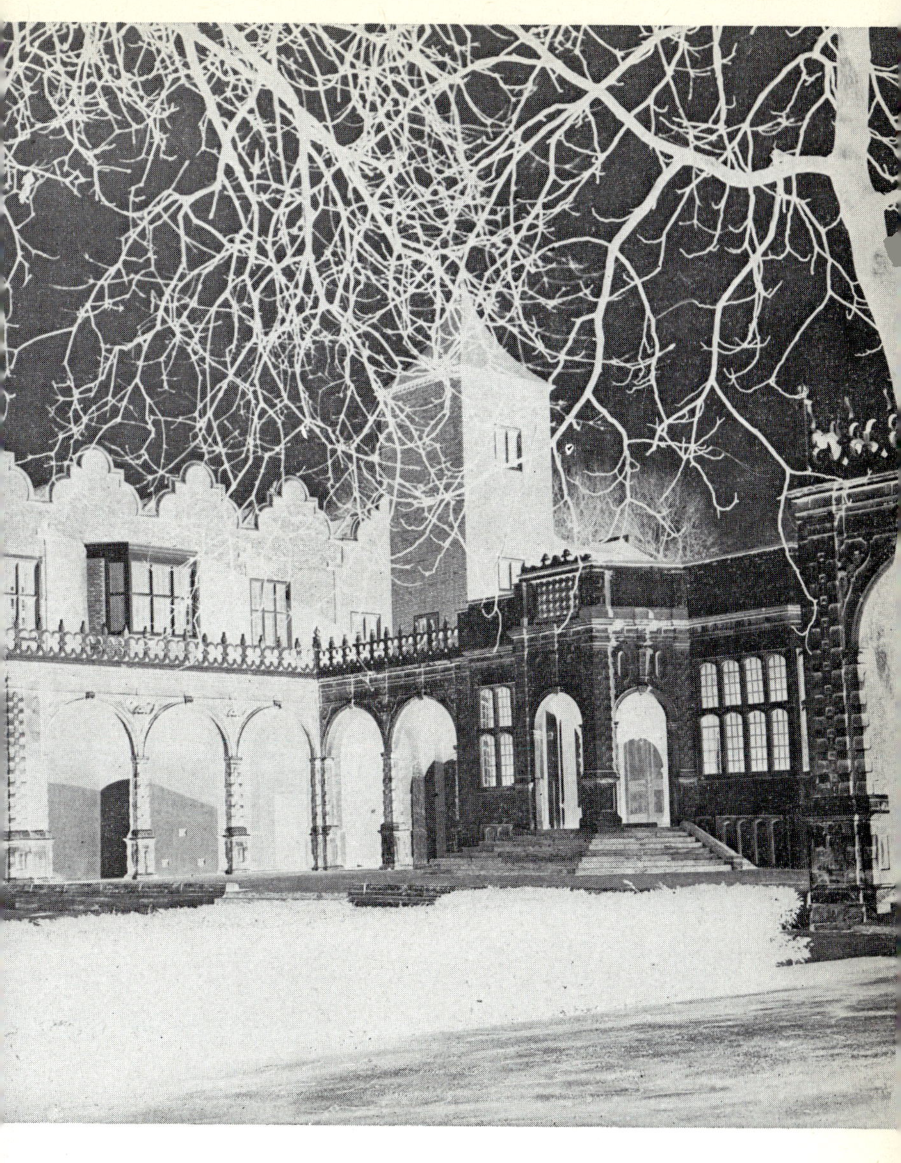

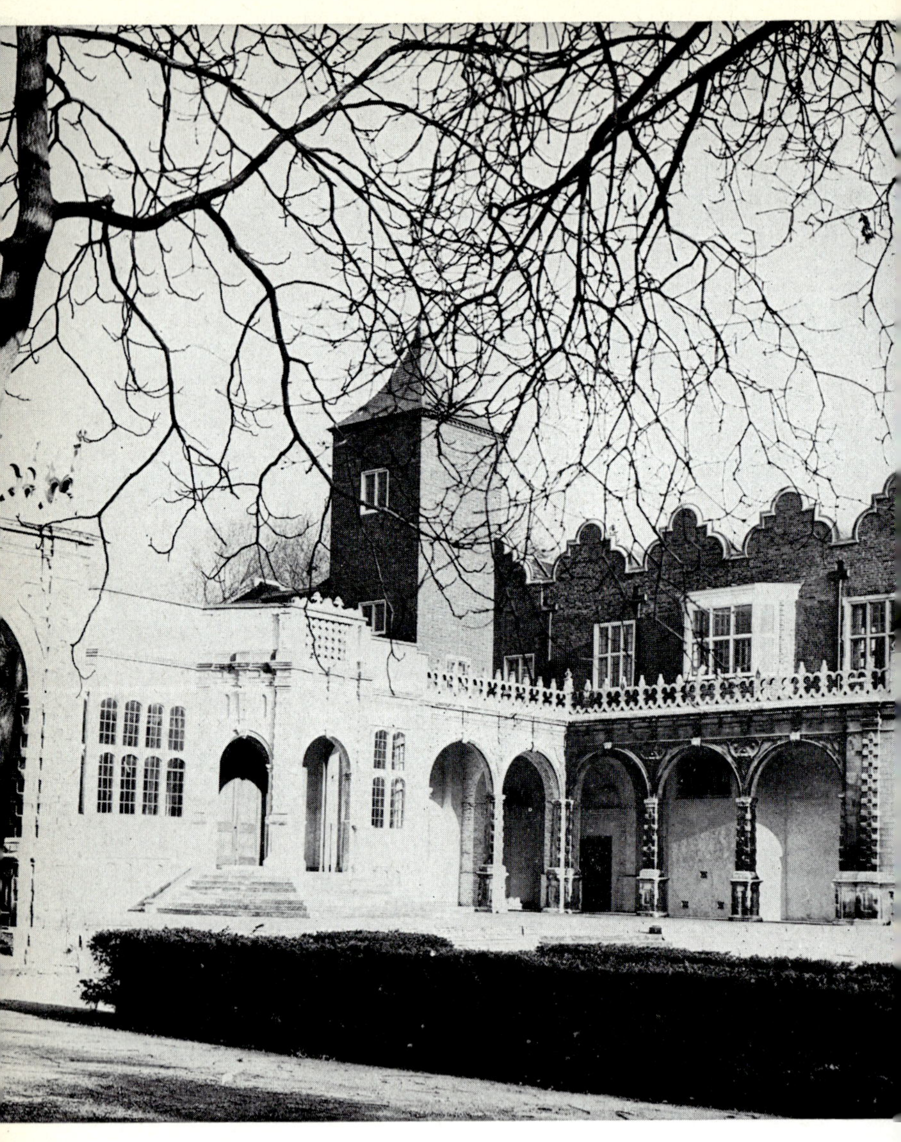

Print from correctly exposed and over-developed negative (opposite)
The print is excessively contrasty and highlight detail has been lost although shadow detail is apparent.

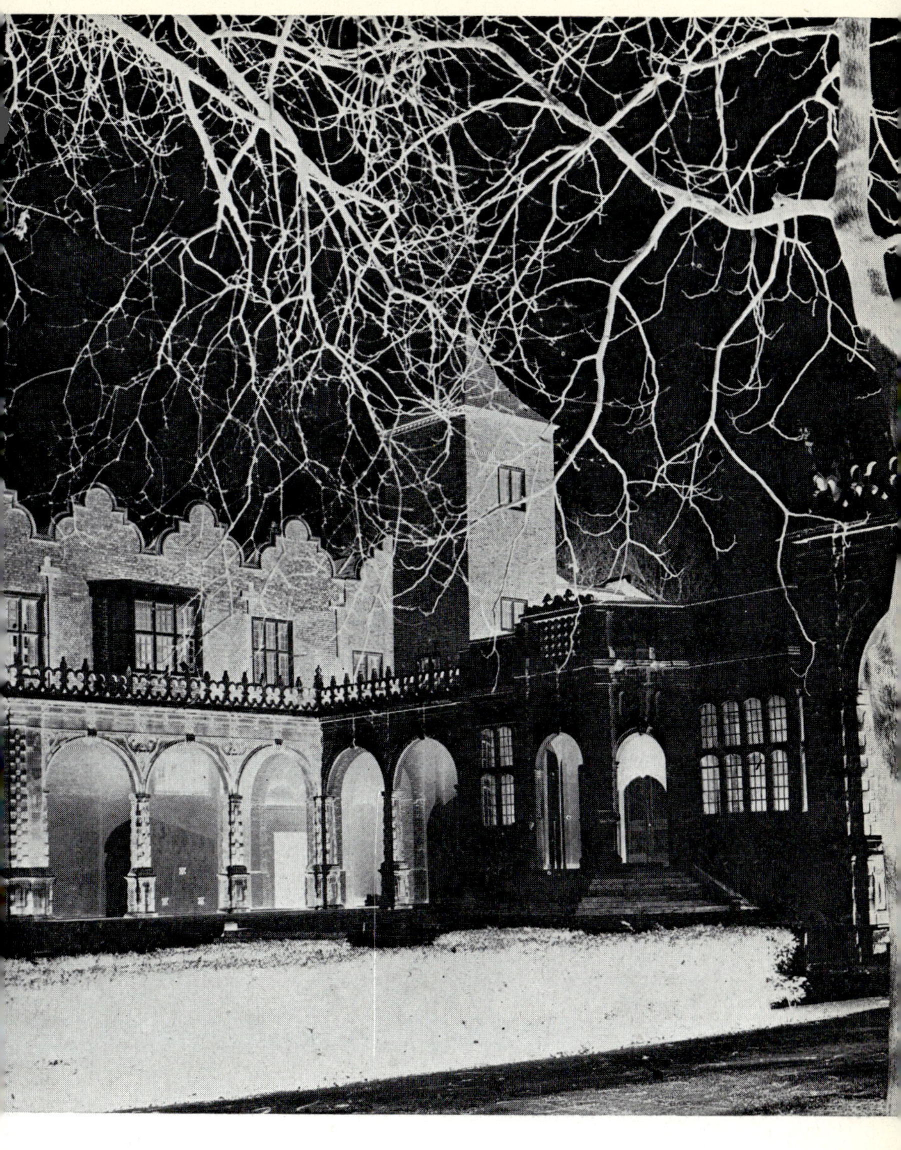

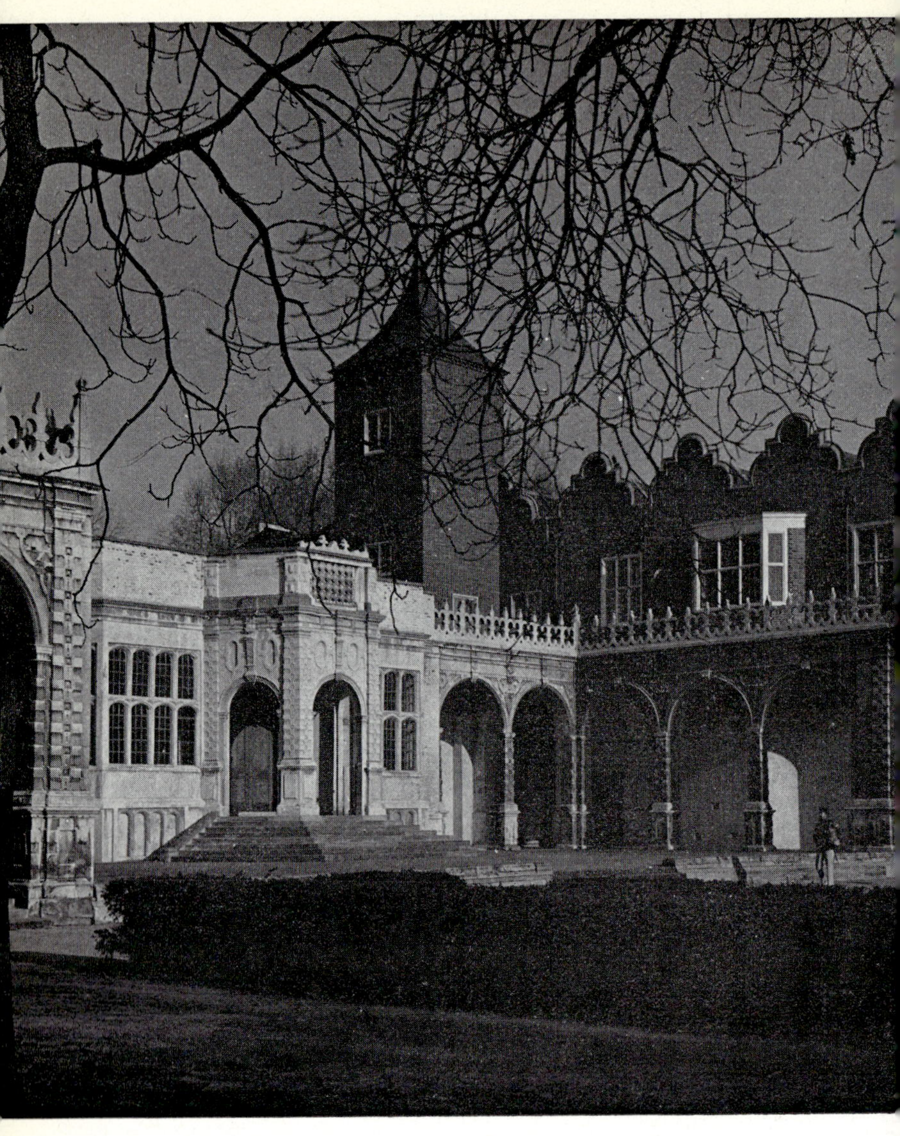

Print from correctly exposed and under-developed negative (opposite)
The print is low in contrast and too dense, but shows some shadow detail.

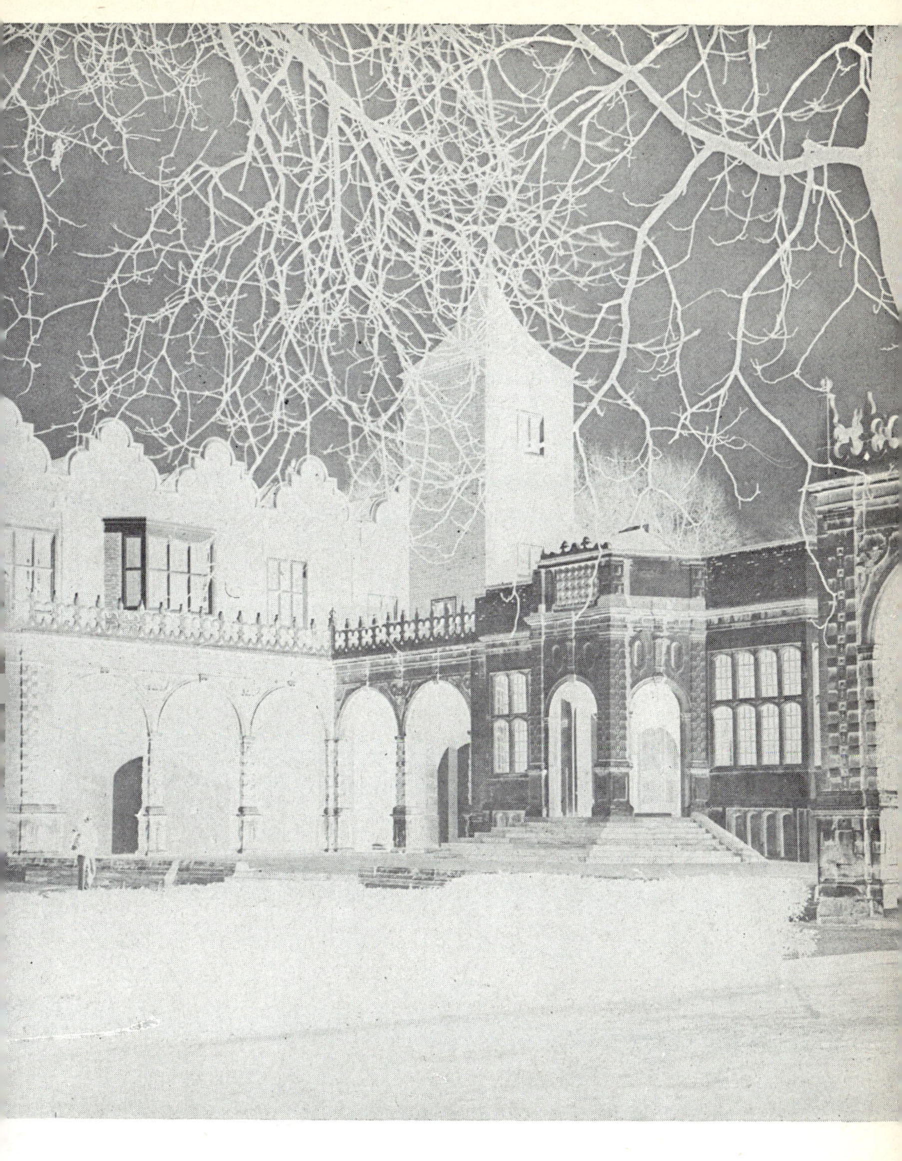

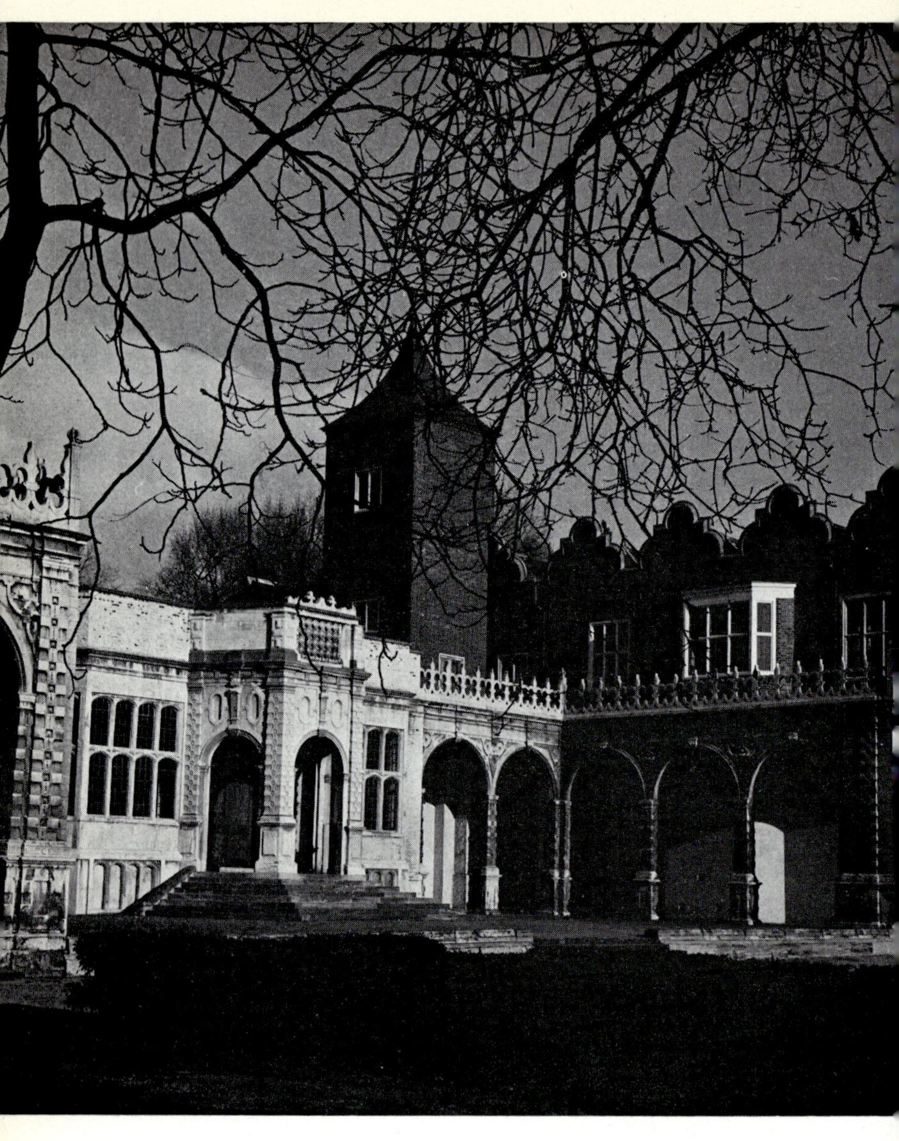

Print from over-exposed and correctly developed negative (opposite)
Although acceptable this print is somewhat lacking in contrast.

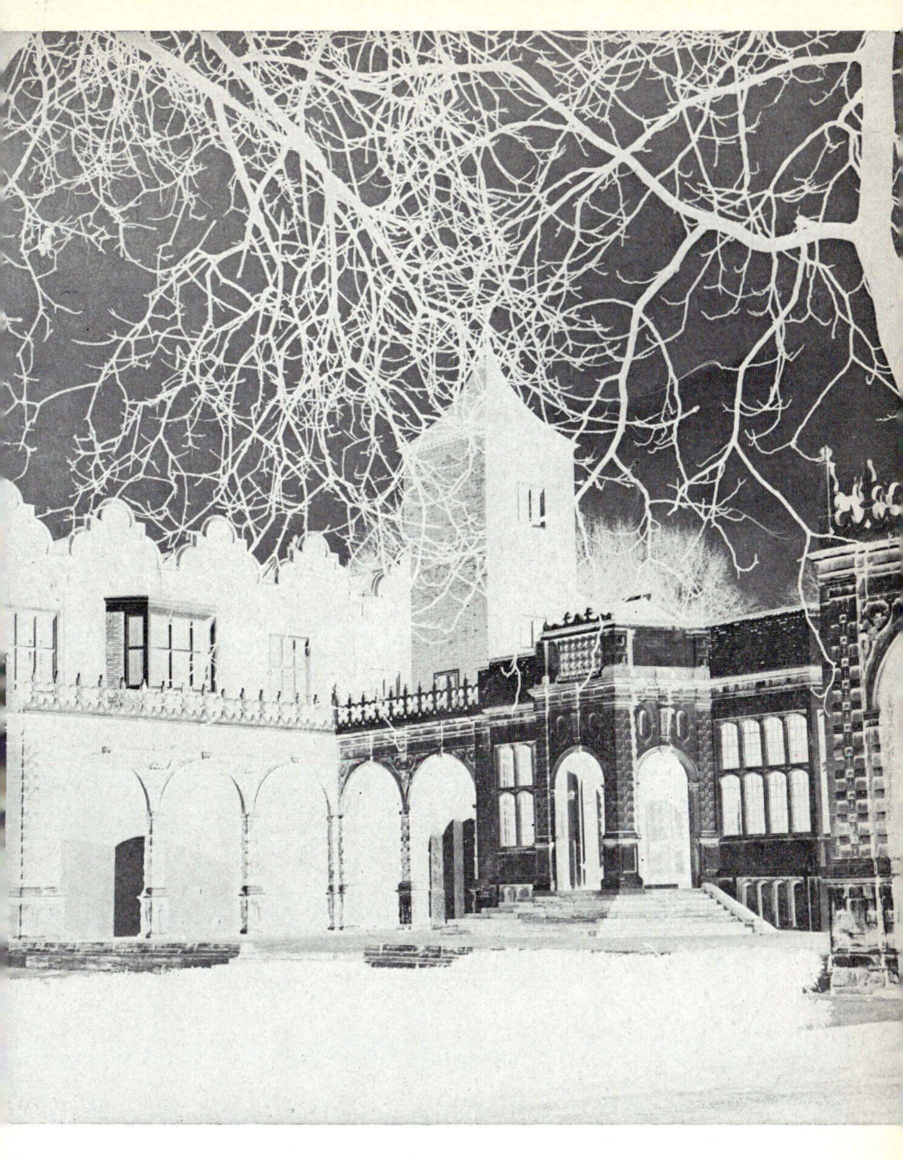

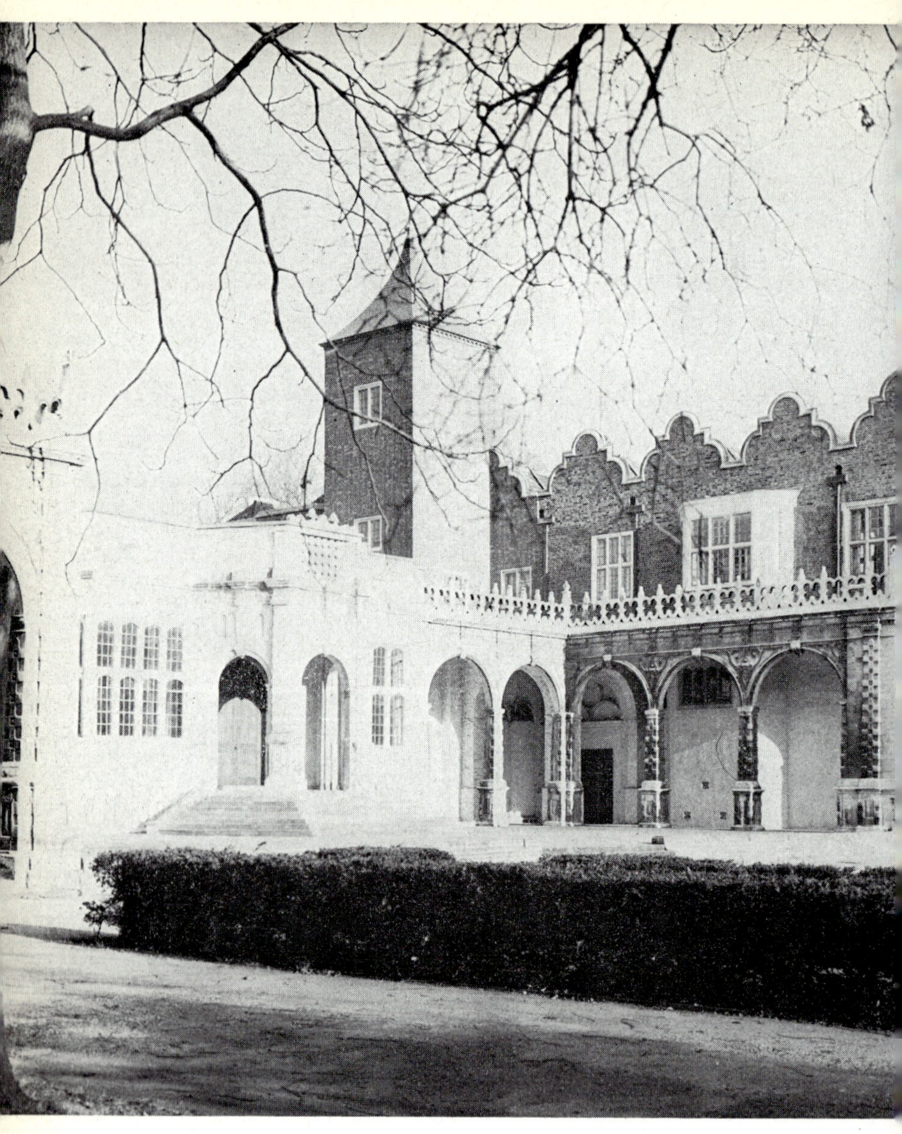

Print from over-exposed and over-developed negative (opposite)
The print is too contrasty and highlight detail has been lost.

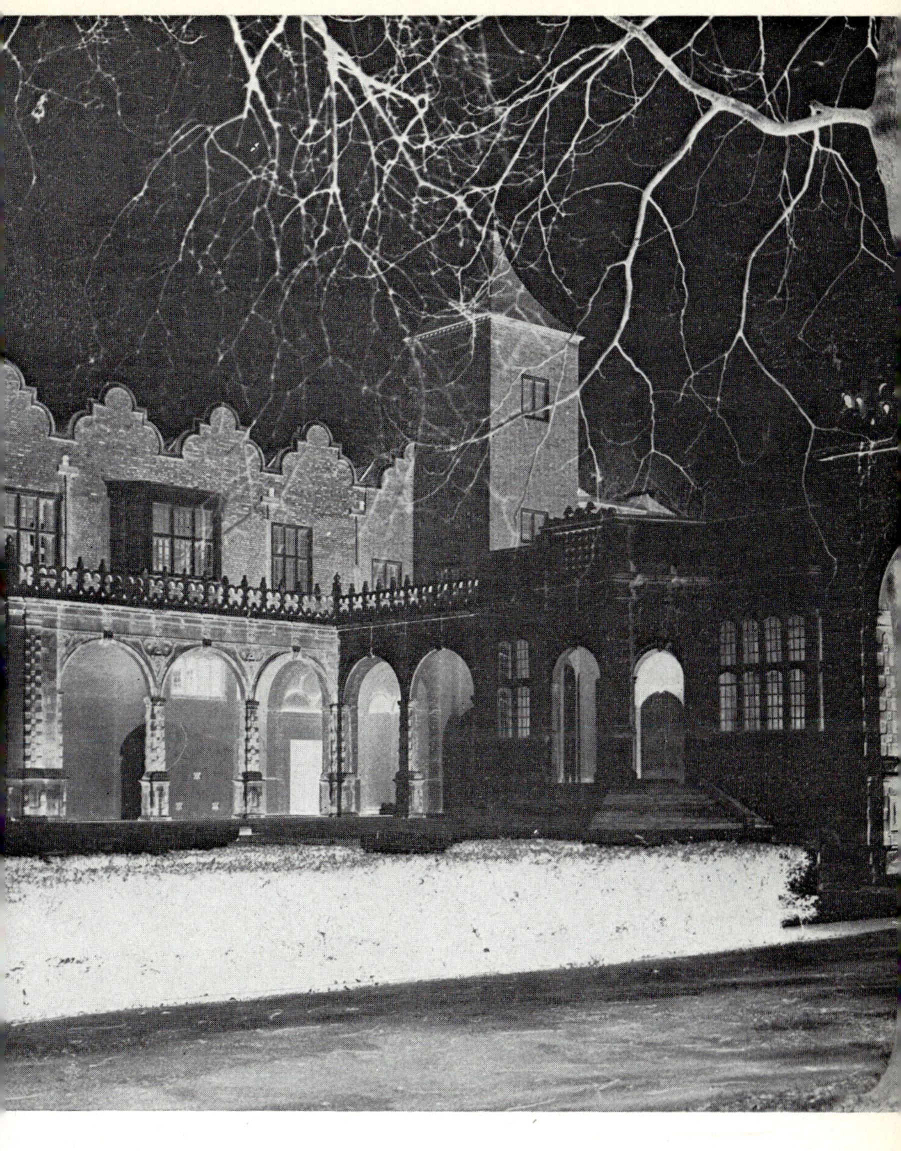

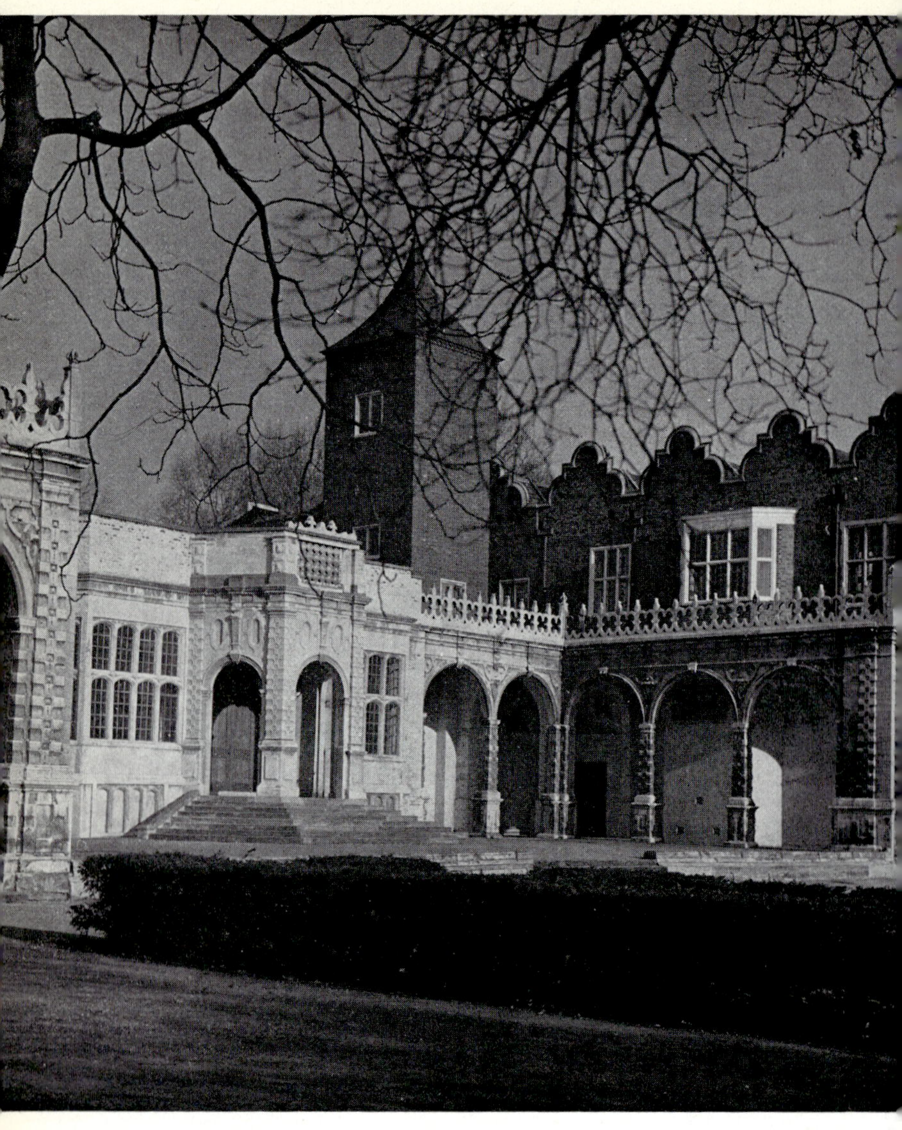

Print from over-exposed and under-developed negative (opposite)
Although both highlight and shadow detail can be seen the print is far too low in contrast.

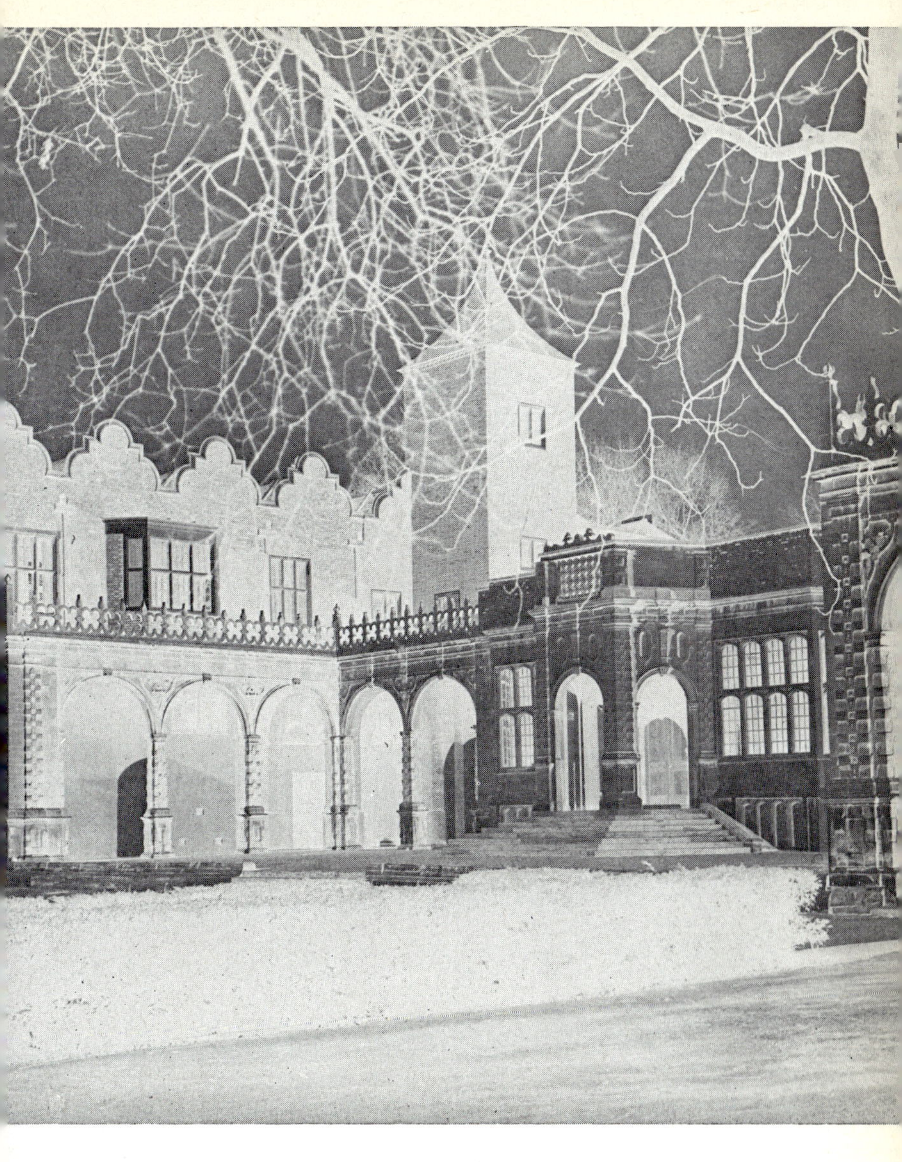

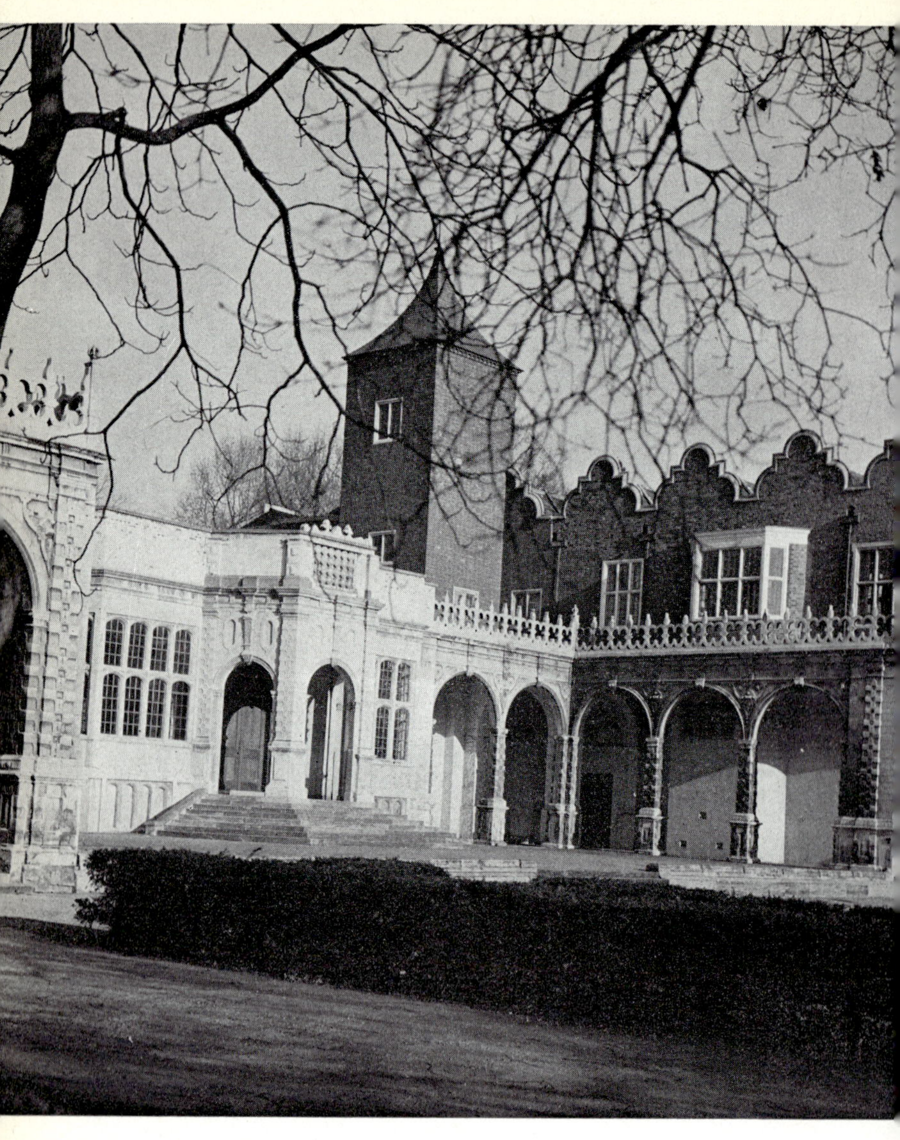

Print from under-exposed and correctly developed negative (opposite)
This print is far too dense and shadow detail is almost absent.

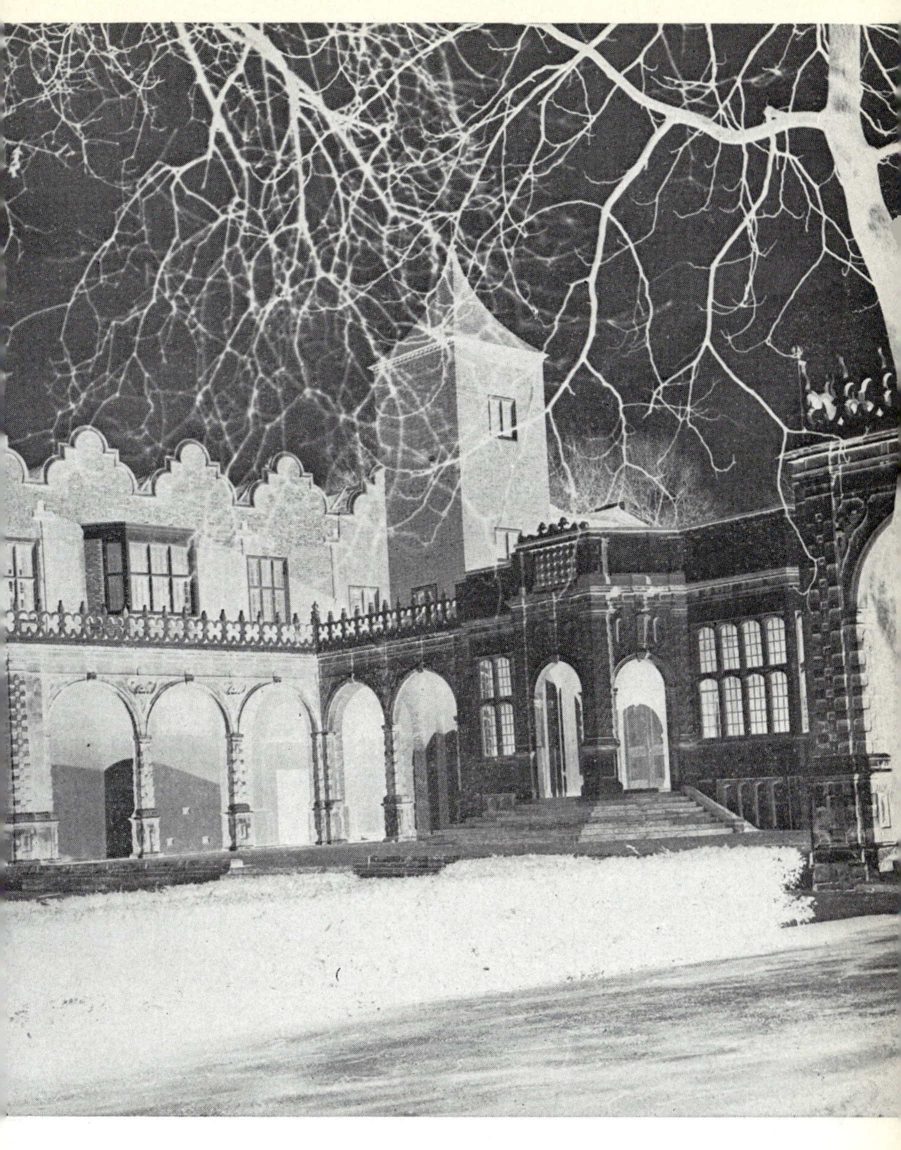

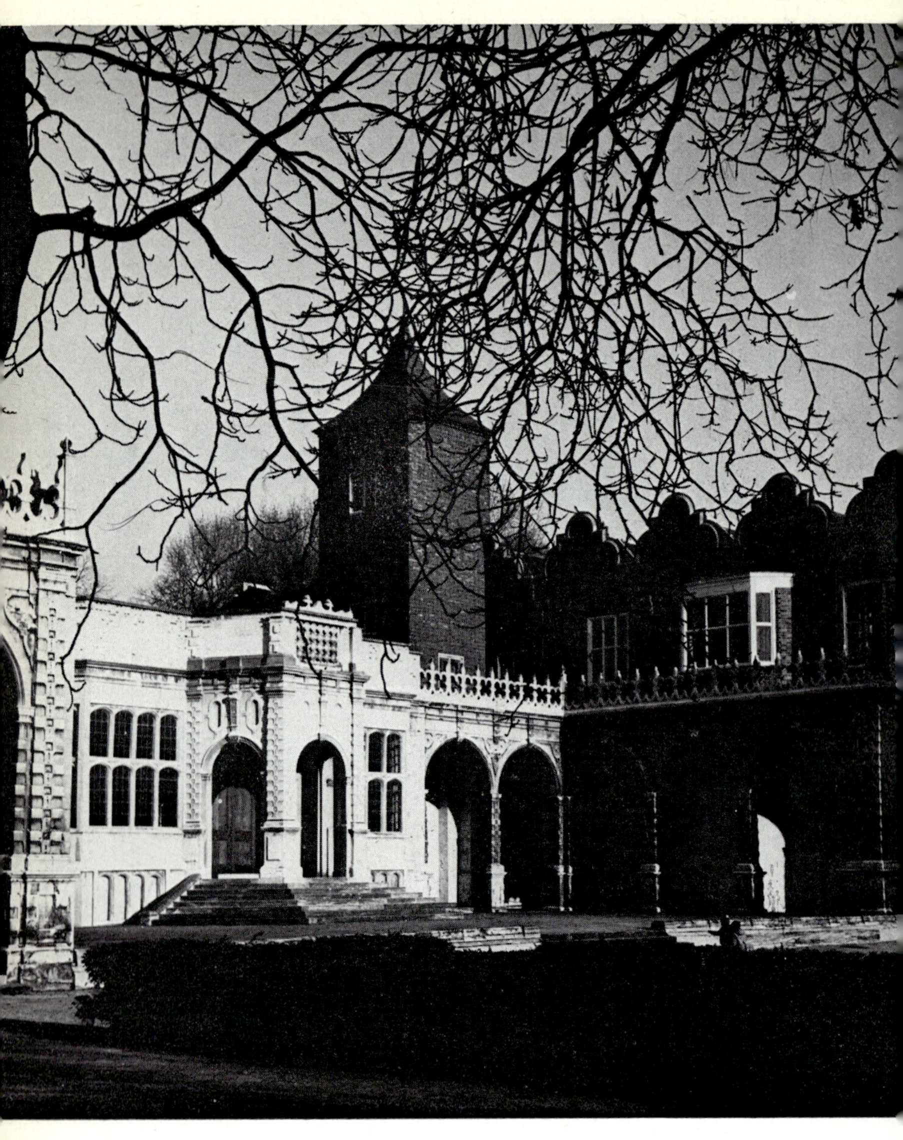

Print from under-exposed and over-developed negative (opposite)
This print is far too contrasty and shadow detail is absent.

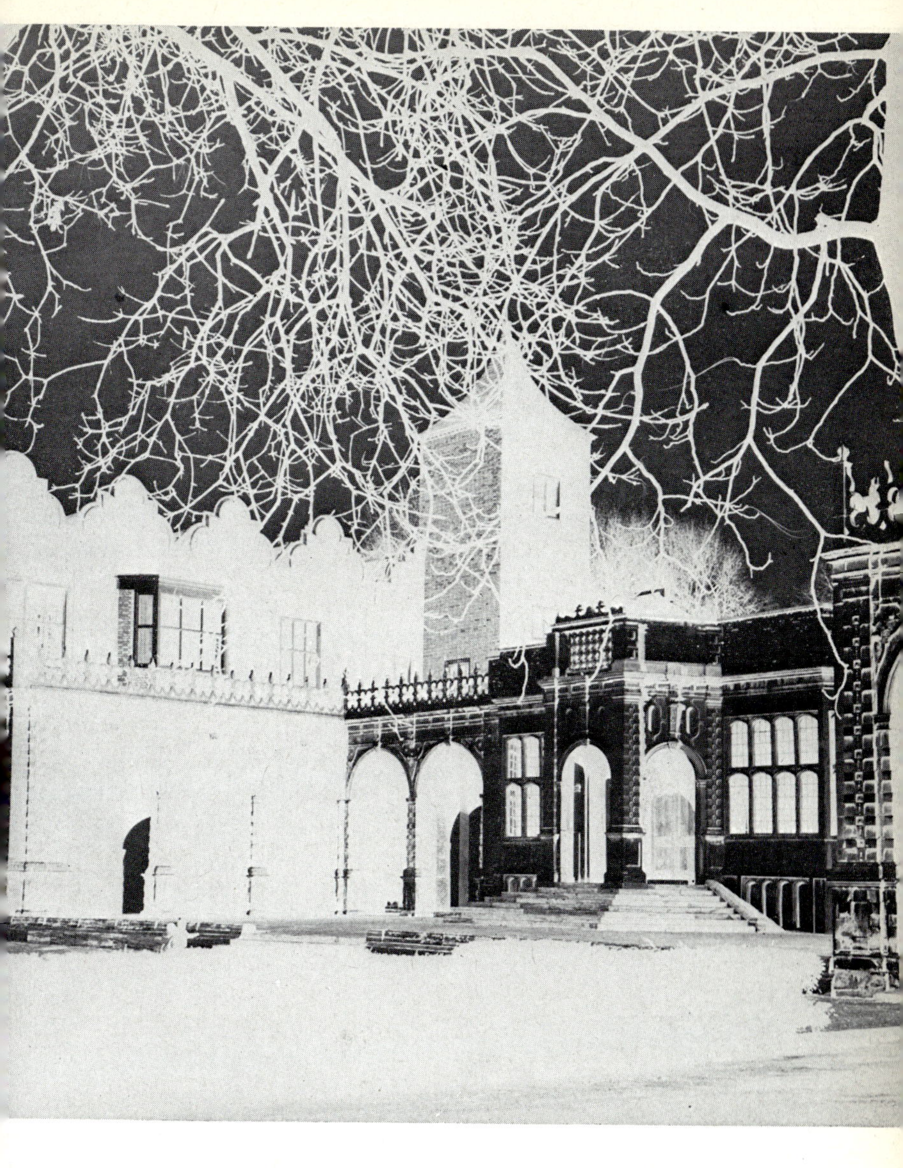

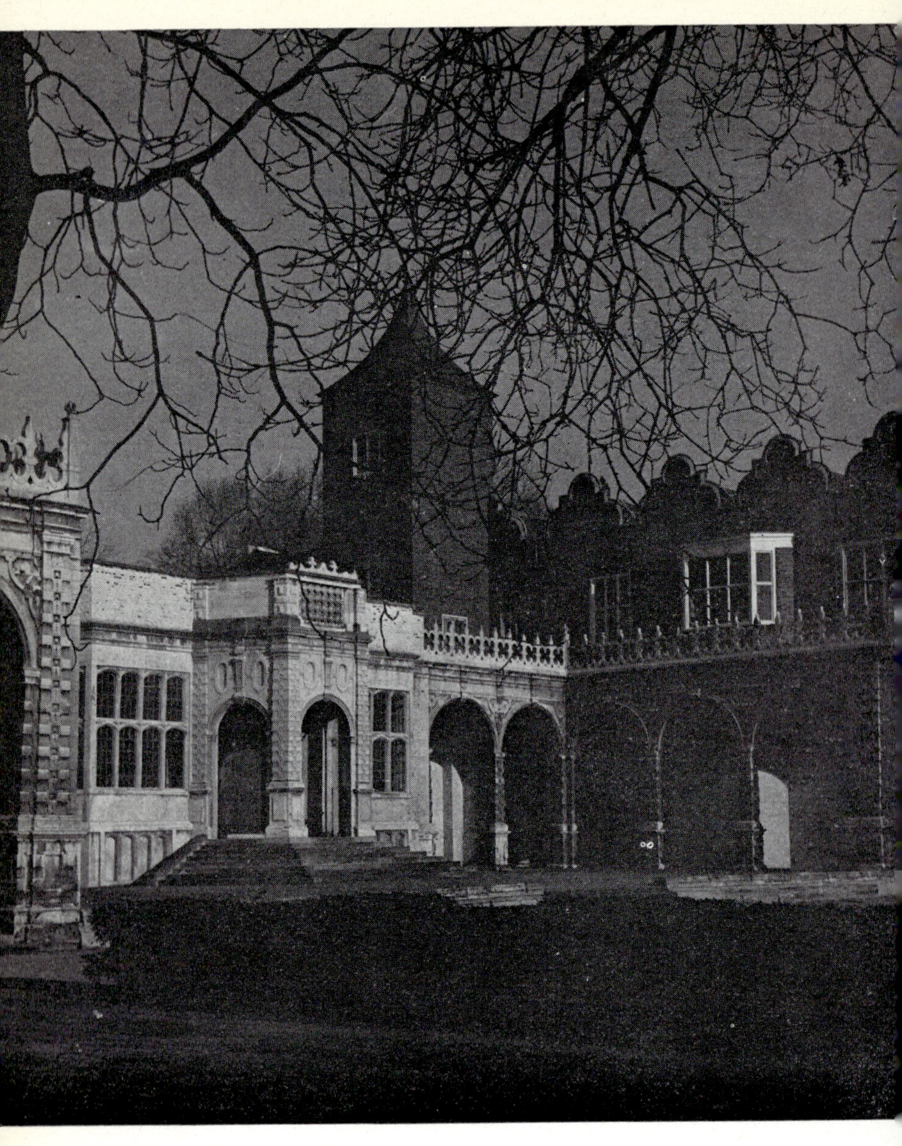

Print from under-exposed and under-developed negative (opposite)
This print is lacking in contrast and shows no shadow detail.

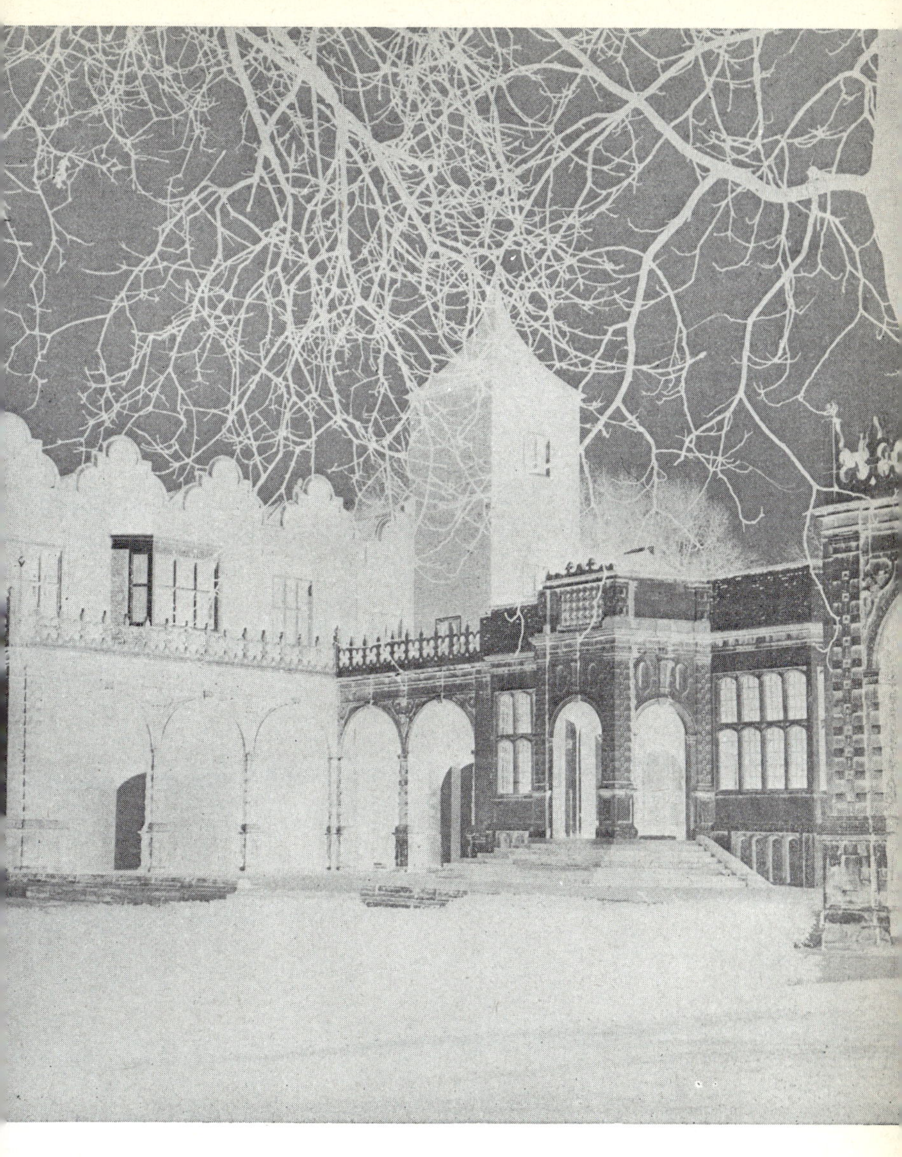

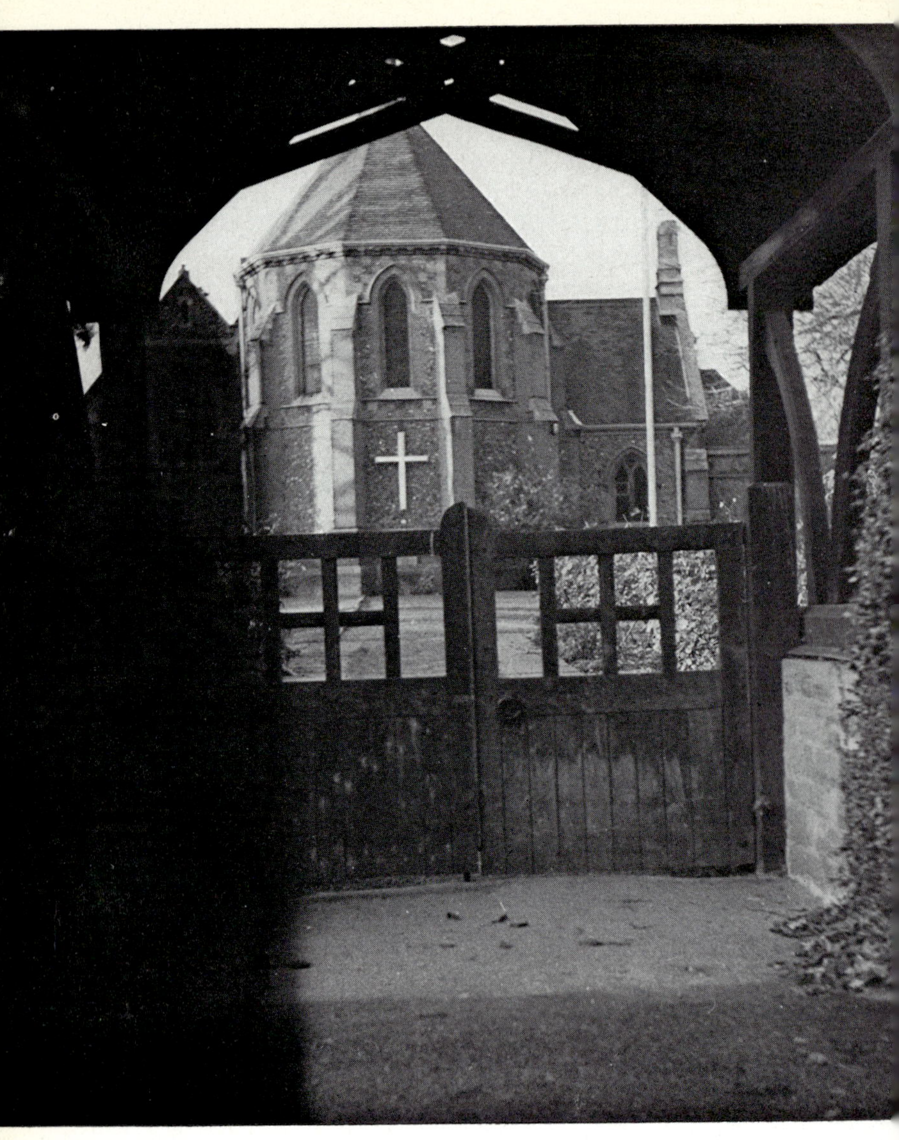

Print from unevenly developed negative (opposite)
The almost undeveloped area of the negative gives a black area on the left hand side of the print.

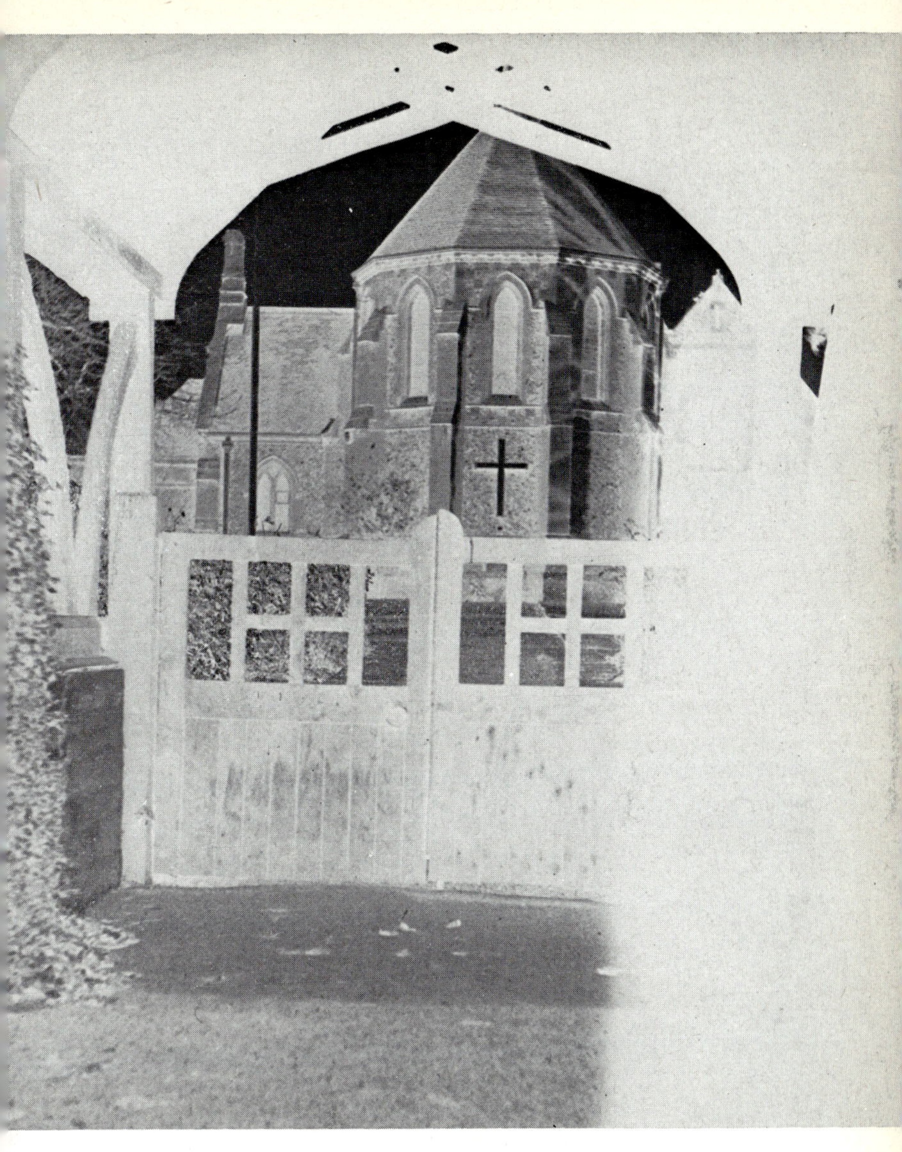

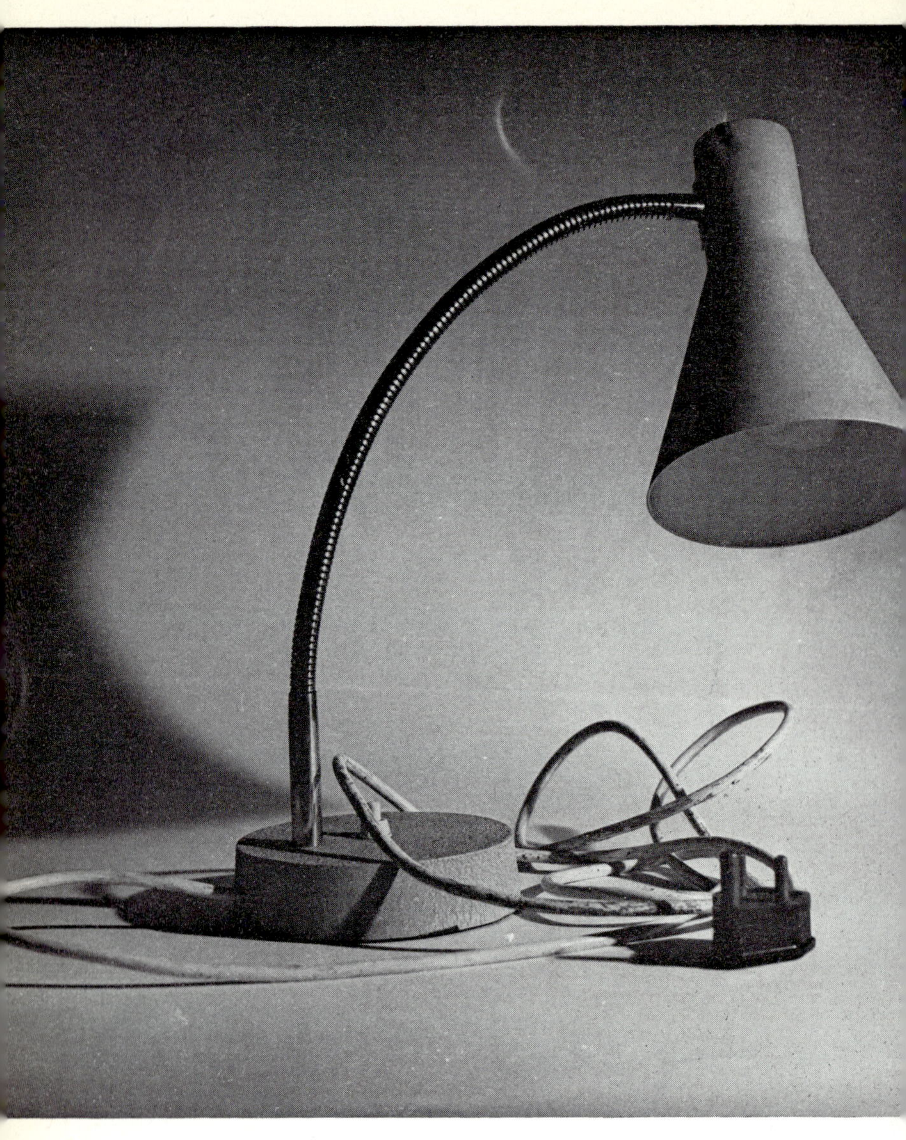

Print from negative with kink marks (opposite)
The crescent-shaped areas of high density in the negative reproduce as light crescent-shaped areas.

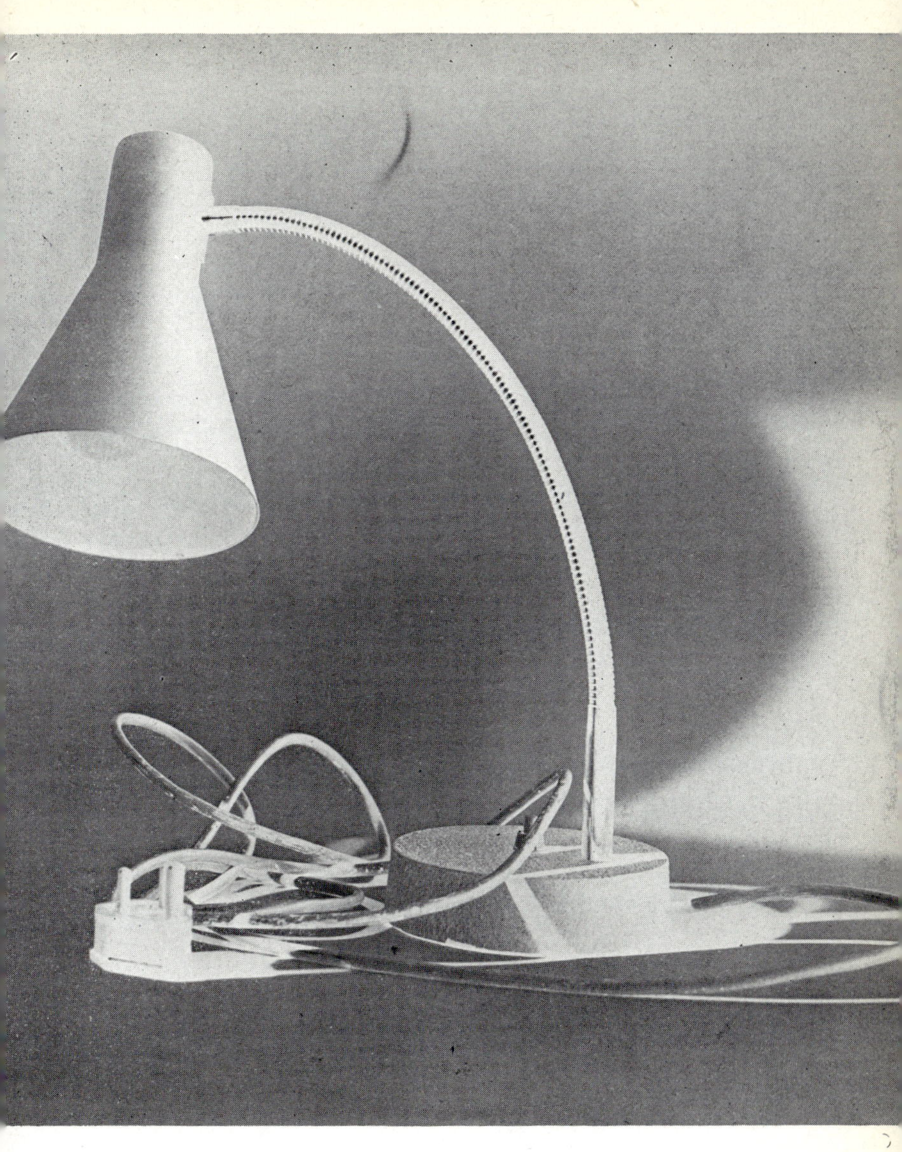

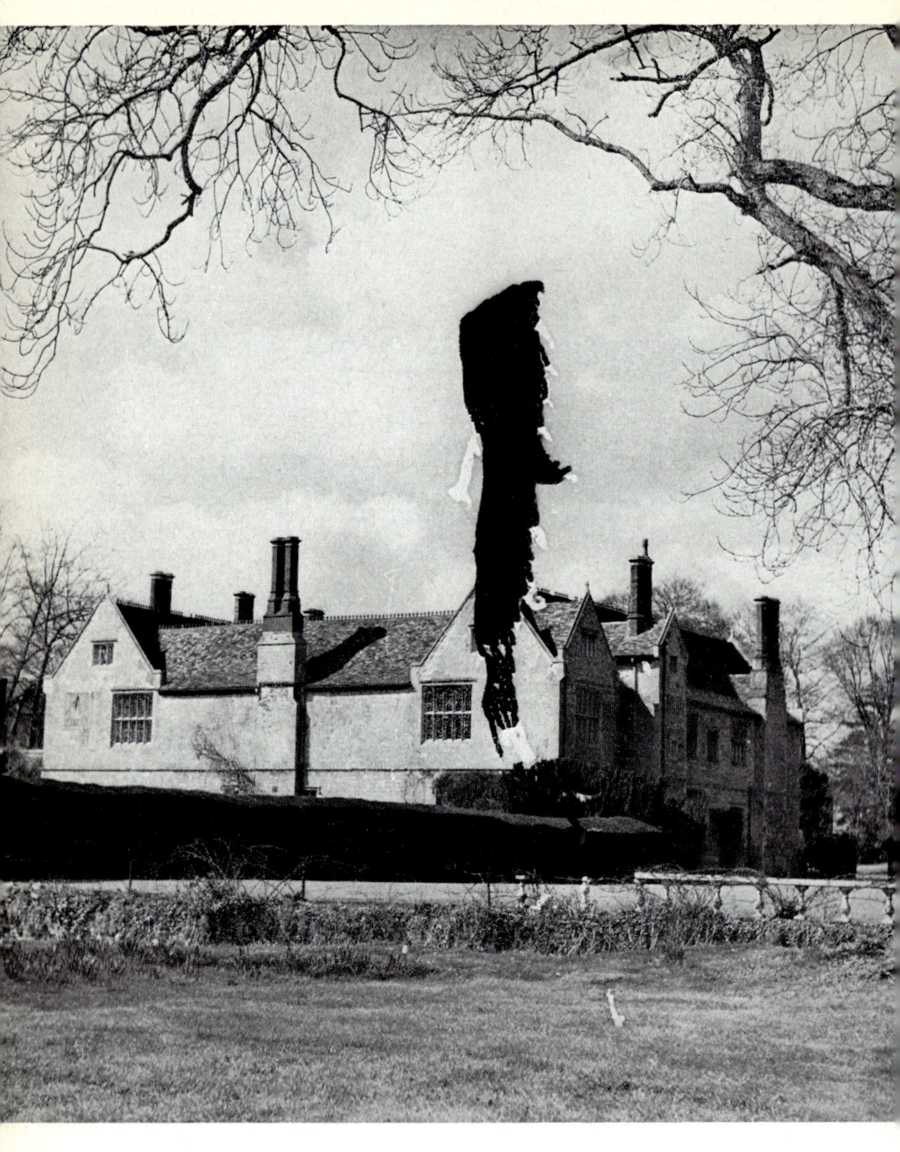

Print from abraded negative (opposite)
The area from which the emulsion was removed in the negative clearly shows as a black area in the print.

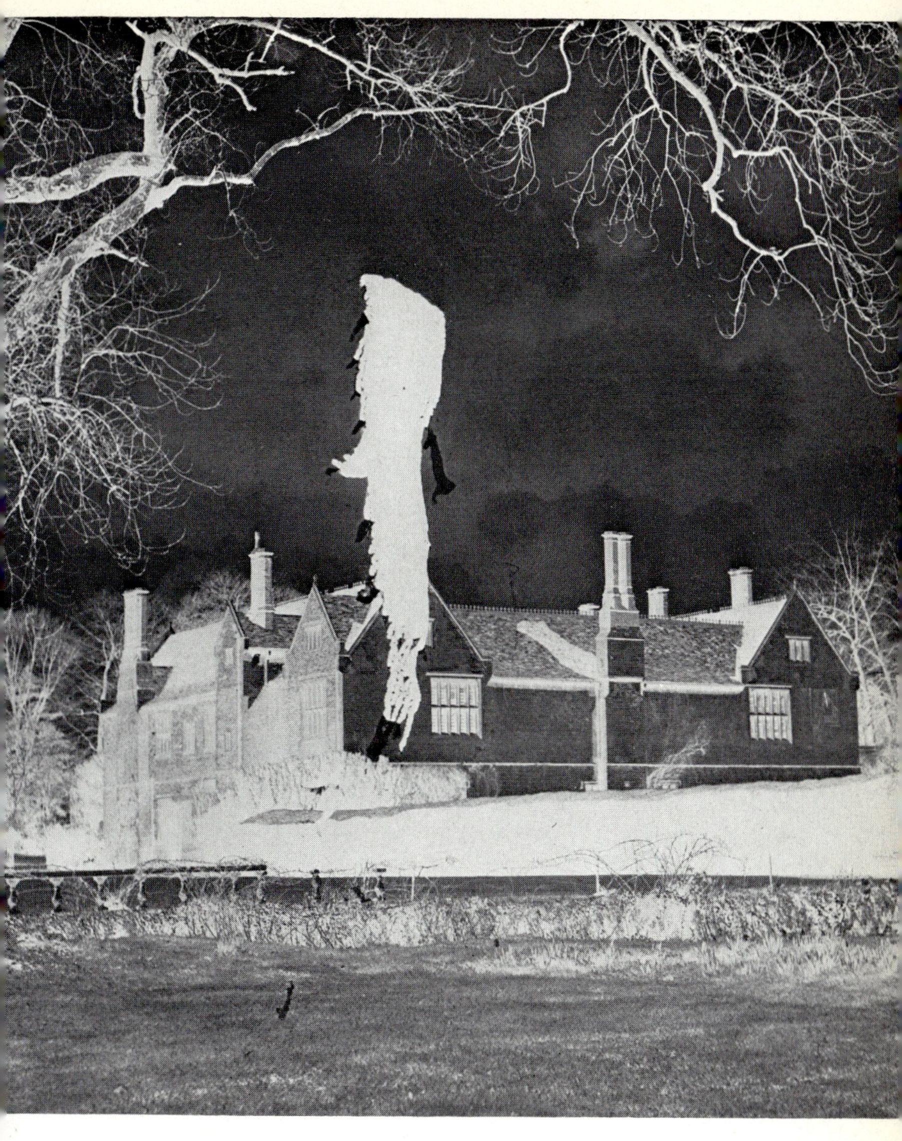

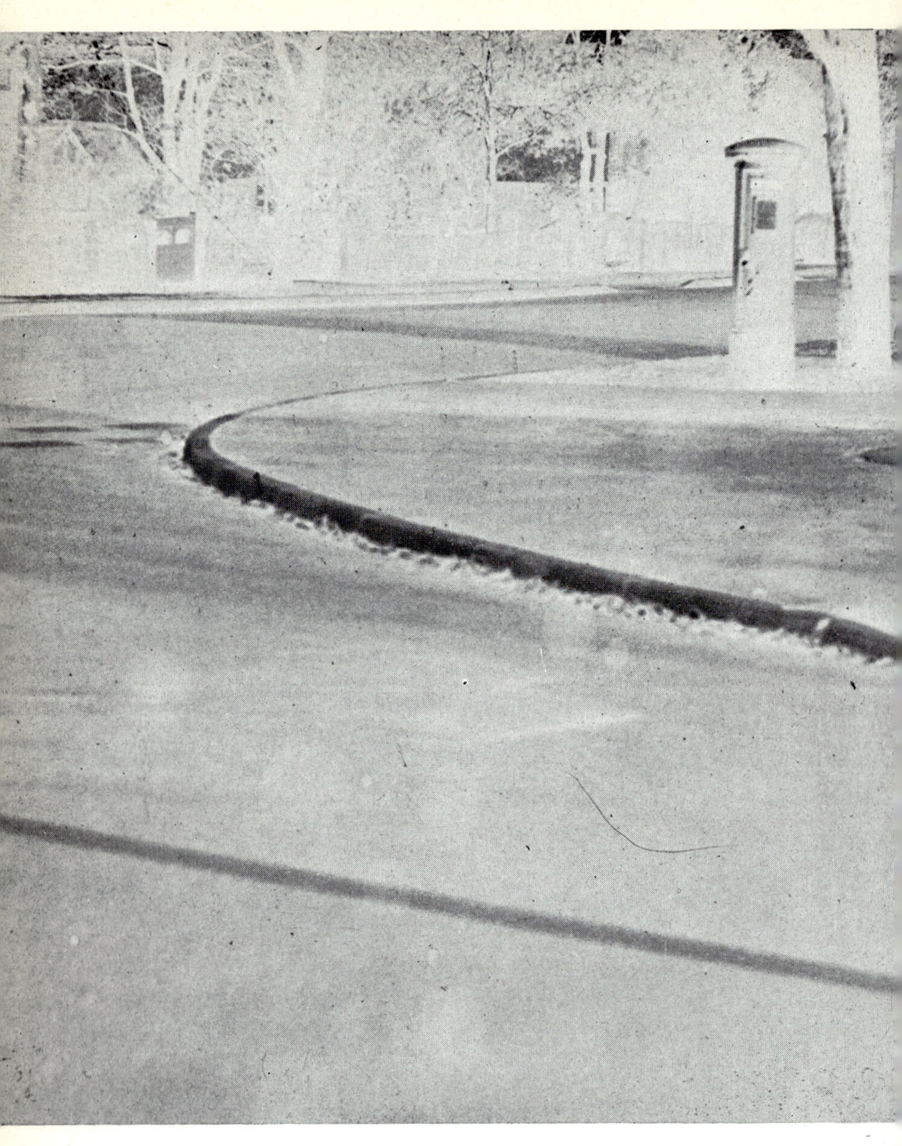

Print from water-splashed negative
An enlarged portion of the negative shows small patches lower in density than their surroundings which reproduce as small dark areas in the print on the facing page.

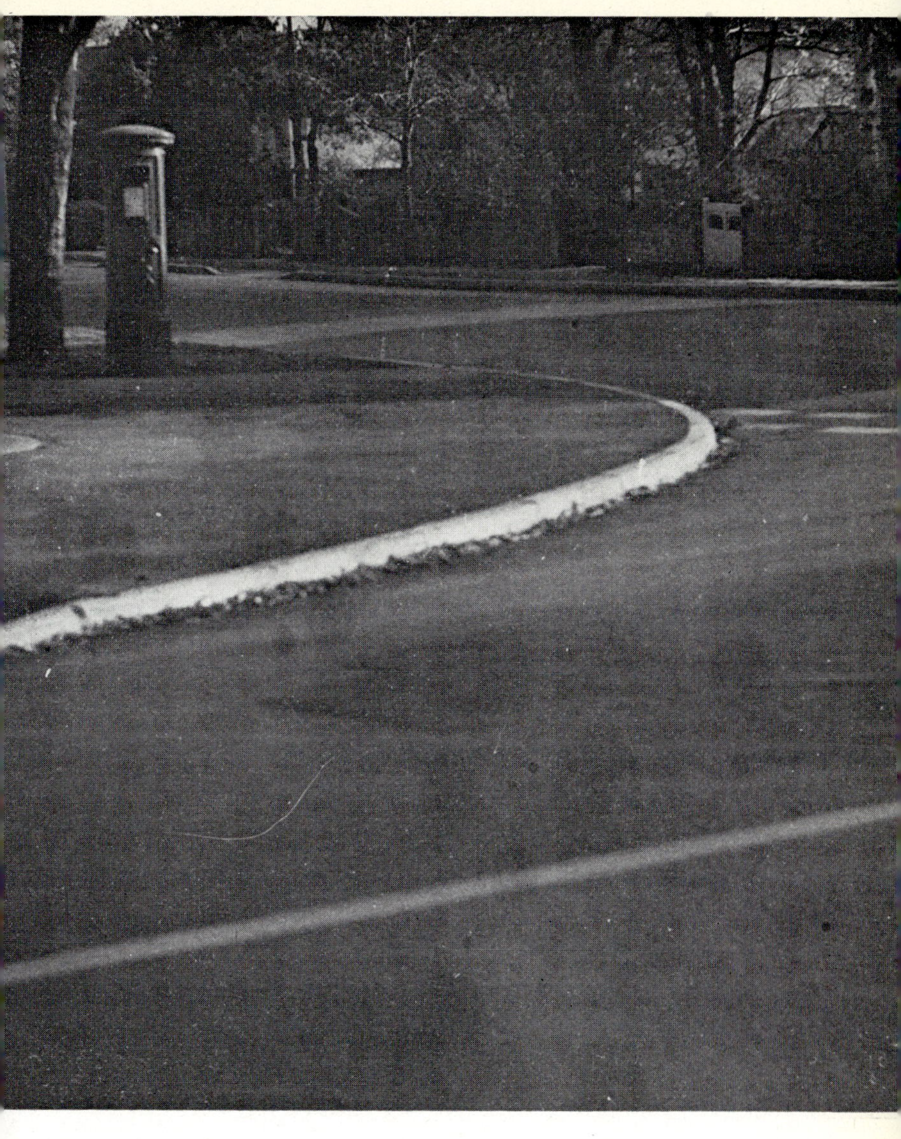

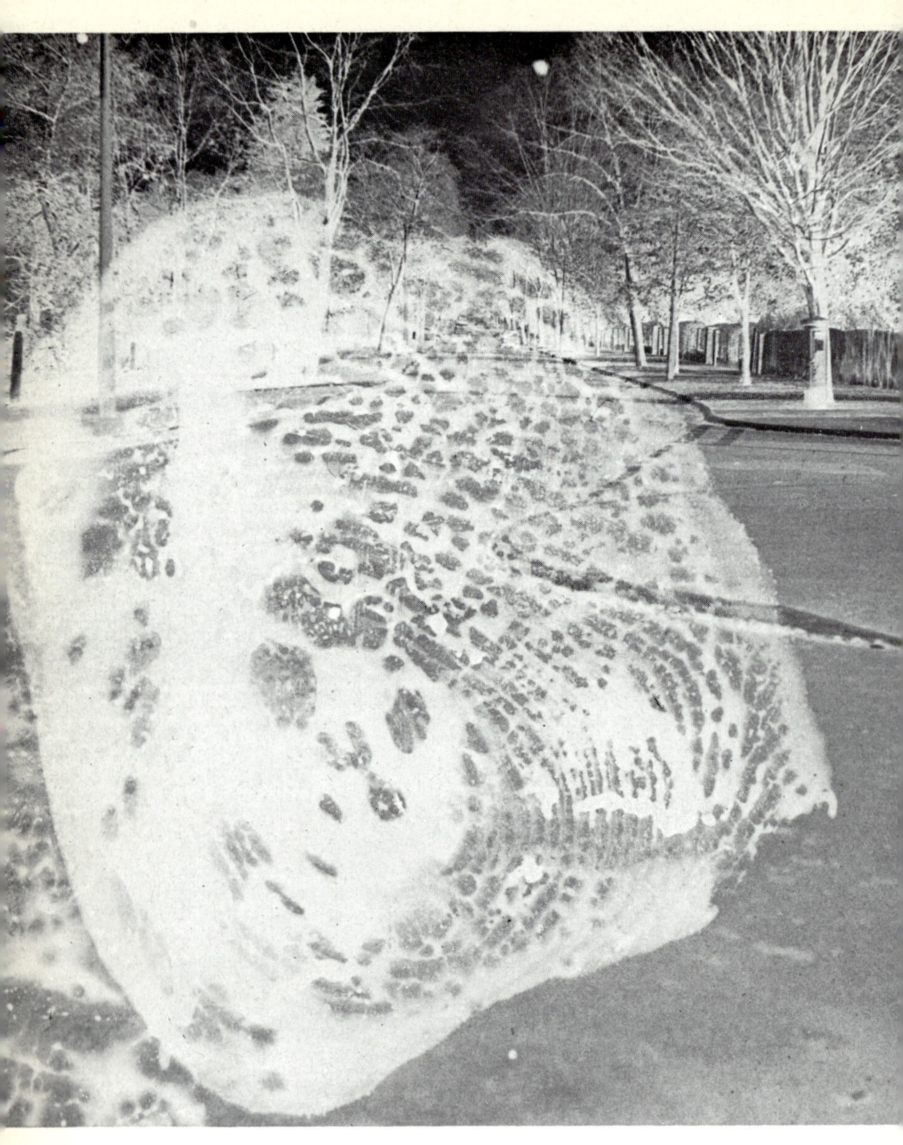

Print from finger-marked negative
The thumb print, clear on the negative, shows as a black print opposite.

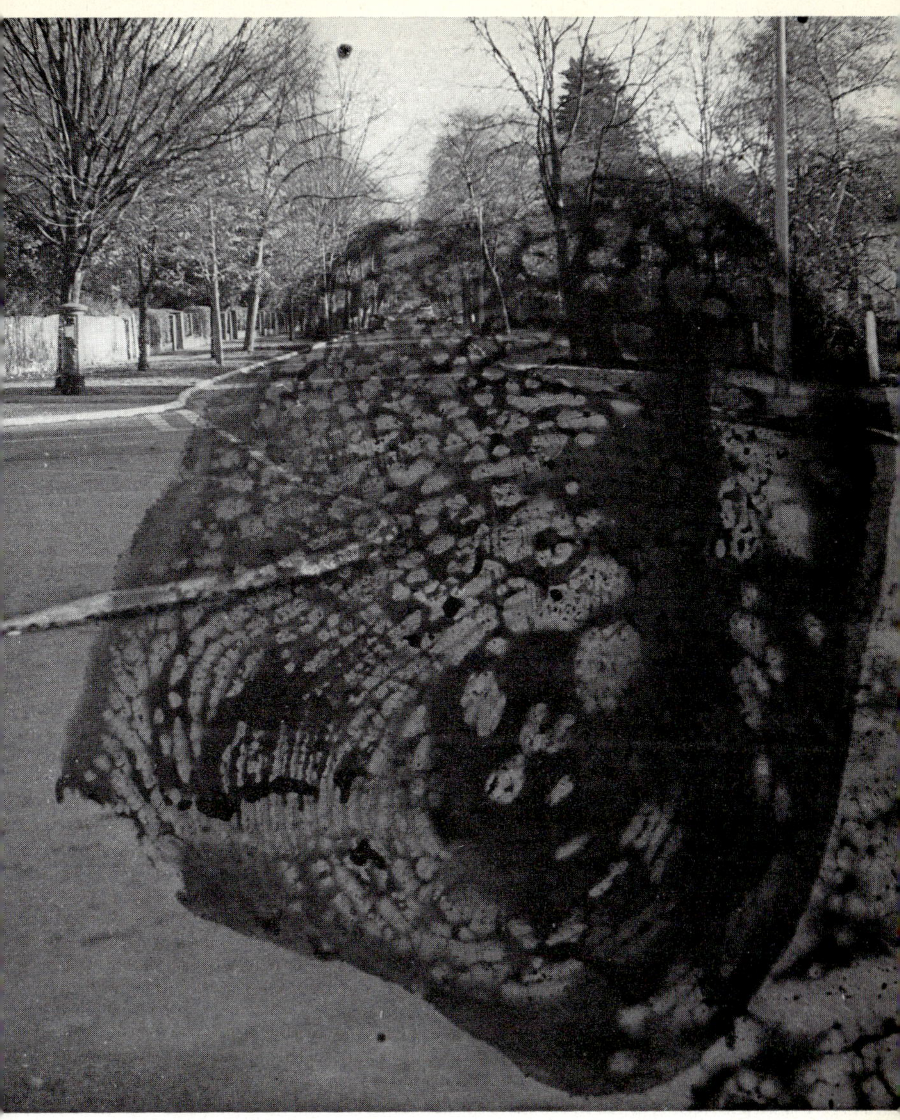

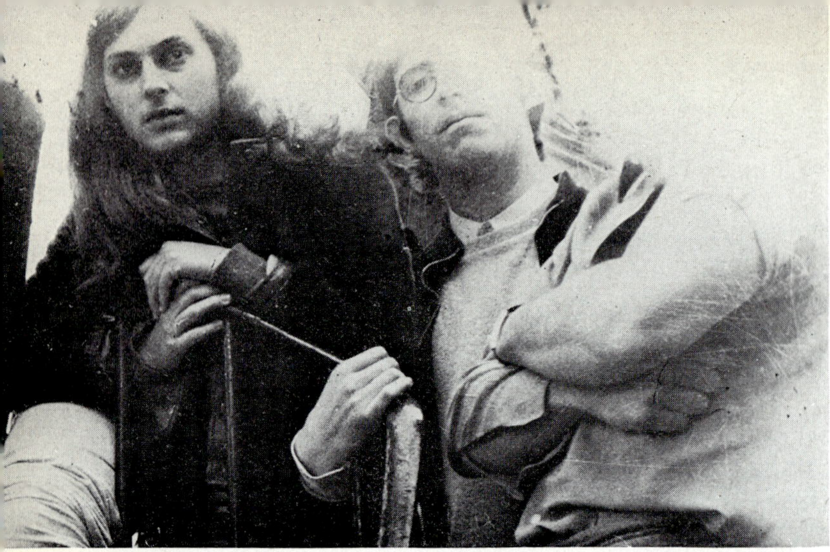

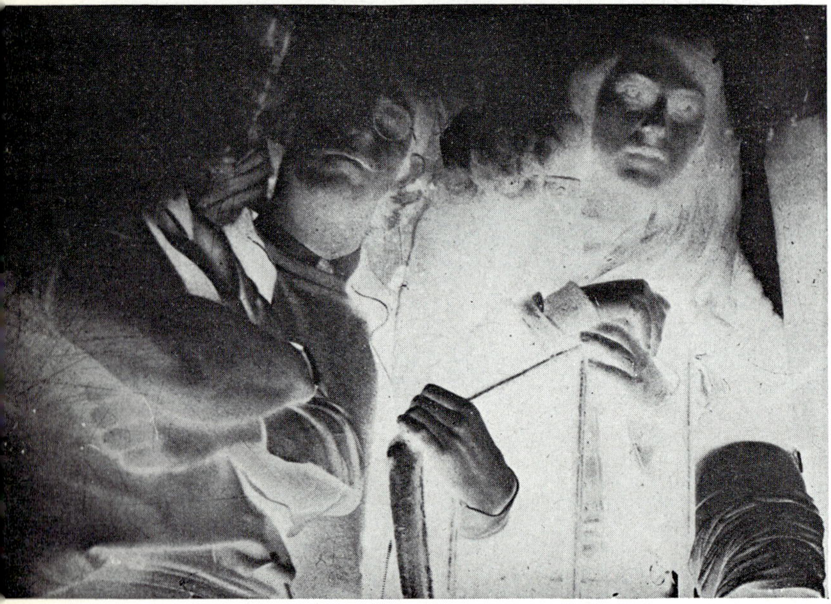

Print from incompletely fixed negative
An enlarged portion of the incompletely fixed negative shows failure to form an image in those areas which were incompletely fixed.

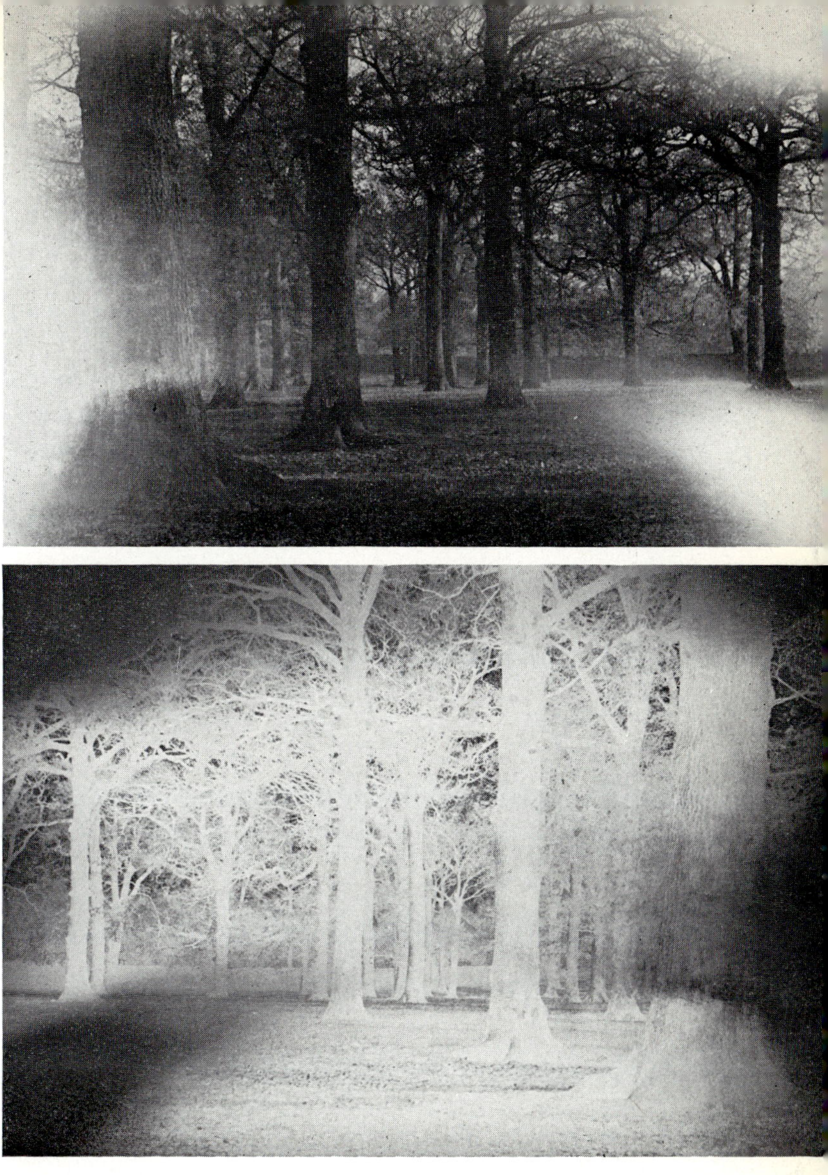

Print from negative with edge fog
The black fogged areas of the negative show up as white areas in the print.

ganate bleach). These products are rendered colourless and soluble by a clearing bath. A solution of metabisulphite or sulphite is normally used for this purpose. The clearing bath chemicals and their reaction products are then removed by washing.

Reversal or second exposure

In order to render the remaining silver halide capable of being developed, it must be exposed to light to form a latent image. Sometimes, it is recommended that for re-exposing the film it is removed from the spiral and exposed to a bright tungsten lamp, e.g. 1 minute at 1 ft. from a 100-watt lamp. This is a somewhat awkward procedure, as it involves unloading the wet film from the spiral and then reloading it for the stages which follow. Reloading the spiral is best accomplished by immersing the film and the spiral in water and rewinding under the surface.

Many modern spirals are translucent, so it is much more convenient to leave the film on the spiral and place it in a white pudding basin filled with water. This results in even exposure and keeps the film cool.

This procedure may require a brighter lamp or placing the film closer to the lamp. Generally, under-exposure to the light source results in a positive that lacks density, and approximately two to four times the recommended exposure can be given without adverse effect. Over-exposure beyond this can lead to highlights that are too dense and foggy.

Second development

Development is now carried out in either the same developer as was used in the first development step or in an active developer that ensures complete development of the re-exposed silver halide. If the first developer is used, the presence of a silver halide solvent may cause some loss in highlight quality.

Some manufacturers recommend that this step be carried out in the dark, although it follows the complete fogging of the film, while other manufacturers recommend that steps following bleaching can be carried out in daylight. In either case, make sure that you follow the directions for your film.

Wash, fix, final wash and dry

Carry out these processes in the conventional way, according to the instructions. Following the second development, processing procedures are the same as those used in negative development.

Summary of procedure

A summary of reversal processing procedures, together with the approximate time for each step, is given in the table below. More exact information on times will be found in the instructions supplied with the processing kit.

BLACK-AND-WHITE REVERSAL PROCESSING

Stage	Approximate time at 20° C or 68F (min)
1. First development	6–12
2. Wash	3–5
3. Bleach	3–5
4. Wash	2–5
5. Clear	2
6. Wash	$\frac{1}{2}$–3
7. Re-exposure	1–3
8. Second development	4–6
9. Wash	1
10. Fix	5–10
11. Wash	15–30
12. Dry	?
Approximate total time (excluding drying)	43–82 minutes

Processing Colour Reversal Films

There are three types of colour reversal film processes that are available for home use. These are the Kodak E-4, E-6 and Agfachrome 41 processes. Although the older type of Ektachrome films, such as Ektachrome-X, that require the E-4 process are gradually being withdrawn there are still available a number of Kodak films that require this process and in addition other manufacturers make films for the process E-4; for example: Cilchrome, Fujichrome R-100 and Professional, Sakuracolor R 100, 3M Color Slide 64 and 100, and Turachrome. The latest generation of Ektachrome films (such as Ektachrome 64 and 200) are processed by the E-6 process which operates at a higher temperature with a shorter process time. It is not possible to interchange these films and processes, and neither process is suitable for processing Kodachrome films.
The Agfachrome process 41 is especially suitable for home use because of its relatively low and easily maintained temperature; but it is a long process when compared with the E-6 process. The Agfachrome process is suitable for processing Agfachrome Professional films which are available non-process paid. In addition to these official processing kits, provided by the film manufacturers, there are alternative chemicals provided by independent manufacturers for both the E-4 and Agfachrome processes. Also the 3M Company offers a processing kit for their Color Slide films. All these processing kits are provided with complete and easy-to-follow instructions, together with shelf life and capacities of the solutions.
It is important to realize that these process kits, like all colour processes, are suitable only for processing the films for which they are intended and should never be used for processing films other than those recommended.

Colour reversal processing procedure

Processing of colour reversal films is the most complex of the processes yet described and involves the steps indicated below. The basic steps were outlined earlier on page 25.
Great care should be exercised in the preparation and use of the processing solutions used for processing colour reversal

films. Certain of the ingredients are either toxic or may cause skin irritation. Accordingly, it is recommended that rubber gloves are worn when these solutions are prepared and used, and that they should never be used in places where food is prepared or stored. These precautions are especially important for hardeners, stabilizers and developers, but all solutions should be treated as if they were potentially hazardous.
It is also essential that the manufactures's instructions regarding the mixing of the chemicals, temperatures of the various baths and the duration of the intermediate rinsing and washing stages are strictly observed.

Preliminary treatment

Before carrying out the first development in the E-4 process, the films are hardened in a pre-hardening bath to decrease the risk of damage to the emulsion. This is necessary in this process because of the relatively high temperatures that are used (about 30°C) which, in the absence of any hardening, would result in damage to, or stripping of, the emulsions from the film base in the subsequent stages. Following the pre-hardener, a neutralizer is used and then a rinse to remove the pre-hardening chemicals from the emulsion. This pre-hardening solution has an irritating vapour; inhalation should be avoided and processing should be carried out in a well-ventilated place.
Films for the E-6 process are hardened in manufacture and so do not need a pre-hardener.

First development

First development is carried out in a specially formulated black-and-white developer which develops the latent image to form a negative silver image. Following development, an acidic stop bath is used which, in the case of the Agfachrome process, is preceded by a rinse. After the stop bath, the film is given a more thorough wash in running water to remove the chemicals from the emulsion.

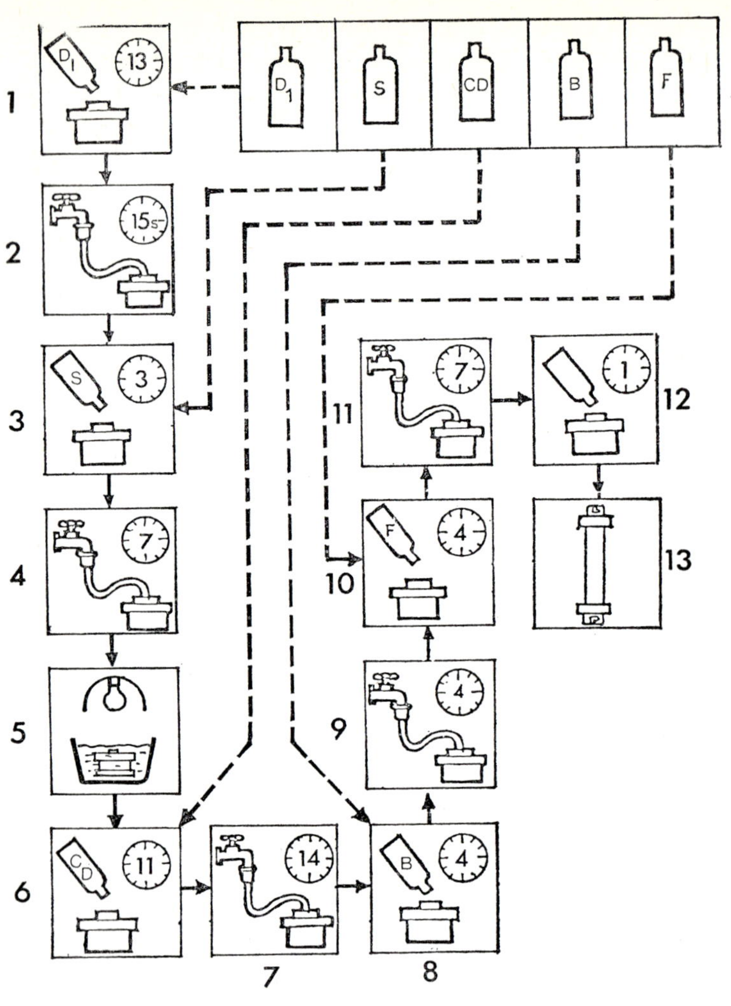

Agfachrome Process 41. 1, Develop 13 minutes at 24°C. 2, Wash 15 seconds. 3, Stop 3 minutes. 4, Wash 7 minutes. 5, Re-expose. 6, Colour develop 11 minutes. 7, Wash 14 minutes. 8, Bleach 4 minutes. 9, Wash 4 minutes. 10, Fix 4 minutes. 11, Wash 7 minutes. 12, Stabilize 1 minute. 13, Dry.

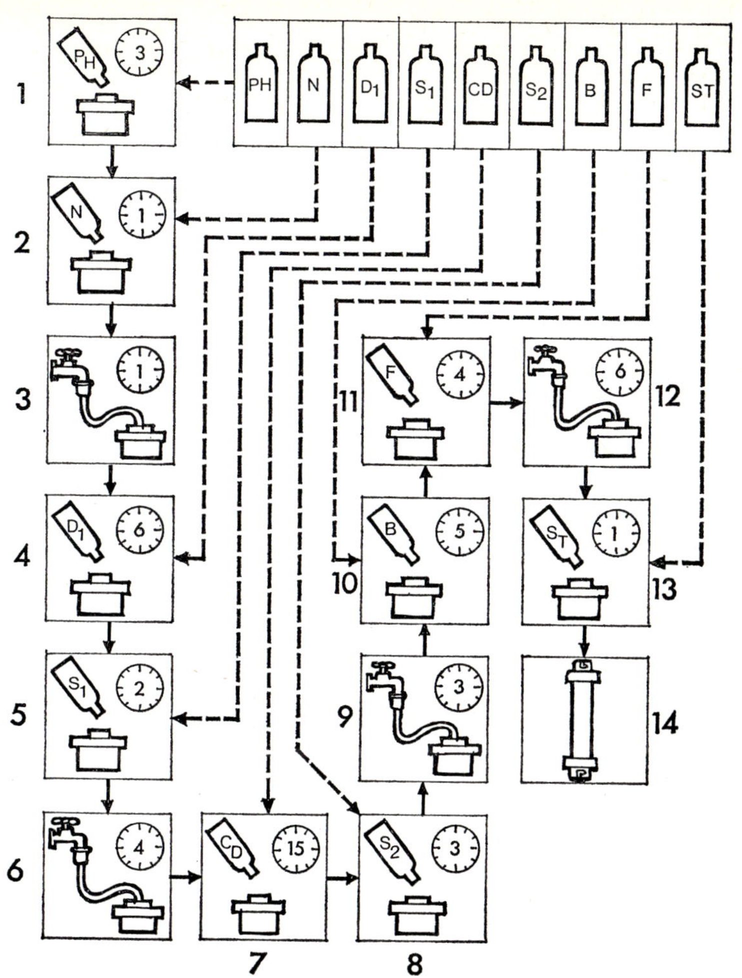

E4 process. 1, Pre-harden 3 minutes 29·5°C. 2, Neutralize 1 minute. 3, Wash 1 minute. 4, First develop 6 minutes 29·5°C. 5, First stop 2 minutes. 6, Wash 4 minutes. 7, Colour develop 15 minutes 28·5–30·5°C. 8, Second stop 3 minutes. 9, Wash 3 minutes. 10, Bleach 5 minutes. 11, Fix 4 minutes. 12, Wash 6 minutes. 13, Stabilise 1 minute. 14, Dry.

Reversal exposure

In the Agfachrome process the film is exposed according to the method given on page 137, using a 500 watt bulb as the light source. If insufficient exposure is given, the final positive image appears very light.
In the case of the E-4 and E-6 processes, no reversal exposure is given. A chemical fogging agent is included in the colour developer formula or reversal bath which has the same effect as the reversal exposure, i.e. it renders the originally unexposed silver halide of the emulsion developable in the colour developer. All steps from now on may be carried out in normal room lighting.

Colour development

The remaining silver halide which received no original exposure in the camera is colour developed to form a positive dye image together with a silver image.
Colour development is next stopped by a stop bath and the film is washed to remove chemicals from the emulsion.
This stop bath is the same as that used for stopping the first development, but for the E-4 process it is important that once it has been used it is not interchanged. The two stop baths should be kept separately and only subsequently used after the particular development for which they were originally used. This must be done to avoid the effects of contamination by the different developers and is essential in the E-4 process because the stop bath is not preceded by a wash. After the stop bath the film is given a brief wash in running water.

Bleach

The bleach has the same function in colour reversal processing as the bleach used in colour negative processing and is of similar composition. Like the bleach used in colour negative processing, it converts the silver that was formed in both the first and colour development stages to silver bromide which can then be removed by fixing. Also, the bleach destroys the yellow filter layer.

Fix, wash, stabilize, dry

Following the above processes, the film is fixed, washed and dried in the conventional manner to yield a positive colour image. In the E-4 process a stabilizer is used before drying which contains a hardening agent that further hardens the film and also stabilizes the dye images. It also contains a wetting agent to ensure even drying. Before drying, Ektachrome films may have an opalescent or milky appearance. This is quite normal and disappears when the film is dry.

The above processing stages represent the general procedures used for colour reversal processing; specific procedures for individual processes may depart slightly from those indicated.

Summary of Procedures

COLOUR REVERSAL PROCESSING

	Agfachrome Process 41			Kodak Ektachrome E-4		
Stage	No.	Time (min)	Temp (°C)	No.	Time (min)	Temp (°C)
Pre-harden	–	–	–	1	3	29·5±0·25
Neutralize	–	–	–	2	1	28·5–30·5
Wash	–	–	–	3	1	28·5–30·5
First development	1	13/14*	24±0·2	4	6–8*	29·5±0·25
Wash	2	15 sec	20–24	–	–	–
Stop	3	3	22–24	5	2	28·5–30·5
Wash	4	7	20–24	6	4	27–32
Re-exposure	5	1**	–	–	–	–
Colour development	6	11	24±0·2	7	15	28·5–30·5
Stop	–	–	–	8	3	28·5–30·5
Wash	7	14	20–24	9	3	27–32
Bleach	8	4	22–24	10	5	28·5–30·5
Wash	9	4	20–24	–	–	–
Fix	10	4	22–24	11	4	28·5–30·5
Wash	11	7	22–24	12	6	27–32
Stabilize	–	–	–	13	1	28·5–30·5
Rinse	12	1	20–24	–	–	–
Dry	13	–	<30	14	–	<45
Total time (excluding drying)		69 minutes 15 seconds			54 minutes	

NOTES

* The first development time is varied according to the number of films that have been processed. Exact times are given in the instructions accompanying the processing kit.

** The recommended procedure is to expose each end of the film spiral at a distance of three feet from a 500 watt lamp for 30 seconds each side, although the technique described on page 129 may be used.

The timing of each step should be started as soon as the solution is poured into the tank. The time of each stage includes a 10 second draining period at the end of each processing step, so start pouring the solution from the tank 10 seconds before the end of the processing time for that stage.

Process E-6 considerations

The E-6 chemicals come in a 2½ litre kit. This is much more expensive than the 2 litre E-4 kit. However, it has one major advantage. All the chemicals are packed as liquids. So you can dilute just the quantity you need each time. The costly component is the bleach. This, though can be reactivated by shaking it in air (i.e. in a half-filled bottle). The solutions, once mixed, have a much longer working life than E-4 chemicals have. Thus, using E-6 at home may not work out quite as expensive as initial calculations imply. The temperature is much higher, so the process times are shorter; making timing even more critical.

PROCEDURE FOR
KODAK EKTACHROME E-6 PROCESS*

Stage	No.	Time (min)	Temp (°C)
First development	1	6¼	38±0·3
Wash	2	2	33–39
Reversal bath	3	2	33–39
Colour development	4	6	38±0·6
Conditioner	5	2	33–39
Bleach	6	6	33–39
Fix	7	4	33–39
Wash	8	4	33–39
Stabilize	9	30 secs	Ambient
Dry	10	–	< 63
Total time (excluding drying)		32 min and 30 secs	

NOTES

* Process applies to new Ektachrome films and final recommended procedure may differ slightly from that given.

All times include a 10 second draining period.

Rapid Processing

The processing times for colour negative and reversal films cannot be shortened and the recommended times and procedures must be strictly adhered to. If attempts are made to decrease the processing times for these films, disappointing results will almost certainly be obtained.
For black-and-white negative films there are a variety of techniques available which can shorten processing times for the various stages. In some cases, a sacrifice in image quality or stability is the price that has to be paid for rapid processing. The techniques given below should be used only if rapid processing is an essential requirement. It is far better to use standard procedures for which successful results are a certainty rather than to use special techniques for obtaining results quickly, only for reasons of impatience.
Before considering specific techniques for rapid processing, it is worth considering the approximate times for the stages involved in processing a typical black-and-white negative film.

NORMAL BLACK-AND-WHITE PROCESSING TIMES

Stage	Approximate time (minutes)
Development	5–10
Rinse or stop bath	1–2
Fixation	10
Wash	30
Dry	30–60

From the above table it can be seen that washing and drying are the most time-consuming stages. Shortening of the times required for these stages would lead to a considerably shorter total processing time.
Washing can be shortened by immersing the film in a hypo eliminator solution after fixation. This reduces the time required for the subsequent washing stage to about five minutes. Drying times can be shortened to a few minutes by the application of heat or by using a rapid drying bath after the final wash.
Times for development and fixation, although not particularly long, may be halved by using specially formulated rapid developing and fixing solutions or by increasing the temperature.

Finally, processing of black-and-white negative films may be carried out rapidly by combining development and fixation in one single step by using a *monobath* The time for this combined step is approximately five minutes.

Shortening drying time

The obvious way to shorten the drying time is to use heat (see page 82). Proprietary film dryers are available which blow filtered and sometimes heated air over the film while it remains on the spiral. Their expense, however, does not usually justify their use by the home-processor.
Drying times can be shortened by using a pre-drying bath of methylated spirits containing 10 to 20 per cent water for 3–4 minutes. Dilution of the methylated spirit with water is usually necessary to prevent attack on the film base. The film may appear slightly milky after drying, but this does not usually interfere with subsequent printing of the negative. Alternatively, the film may be immersed in a pre-drying bath of a saturated solution of magnesium sulphate (Epsom salts) for half a minute, followed by drying for a few seconds in a rapid current of air after removing excess solution with a film wiper. However, with this method disintegration of the emulsion may occur on storage. Both these methods lead to some sacrifice in image quality and permanence and should only be used if rapid drying is an essential requirement. It is better to be patient and obtain reliable results.

Shortening washing time

The time for washing films may be reduced by using a hypo eliminator. Following fixation, the film is given a brief rinse in water and then immersed in a hypo eliminator solution for a minute or so before the final wash, which is now shortened to about five minutes. However, it should be emphasised that hypo eliminators do not remove hypo from the film but convert sodium thiosulphate to other compounds which are supposedly less harmful to the image and therefore require less washing as they need not be completely removed. A good way for decreasing washing times to about one-sixth of that normally required, without any possibility of harmful effects, is by immersion of the film in a 2 per cent solution of anhydrous sodium sulphite for 2 minutes before the final wash.

Shortening fixing time

Rapid fixing baths are supplied by most photographic manufacturers. These usually contain ammonium thiosulphate as the fixing agent in place of sodium thiosulphate (hypo) and have a more rapid fixing action than sodium thiosulphate. Rapid fixing baths can be used with complete safety, and if the temperature is increased to about 24°C a fixing time of about a minute or so can be achieved.

Shortening developing time

Developing times can be shortened by using a higher temperature than the normal temperature of about 20°C. From the time-temperature chart on page 69, it can be seen that a ten-minute development time at 68°F (20°C) can be shortened to 6½ minutes by developing at 75°F (24°C). Few materials will be able to withstand temperatures above 24°C (see page 148).

Using monobaths

With the exception of rapid fixing baths, the previously mentioned means of shortening processing times should only be used as the last resort, because they almost invariably result in loss of image quality and/or stability of the negative image. Kodak Ltd. publish details of a very simple procedure for the rapid daylight processing of 35 mm film, using a monobath solution which requires neither a darkroom nor a developing tank. Complete details are given in the Kodak publication, *Record Photography in the Classroom.*

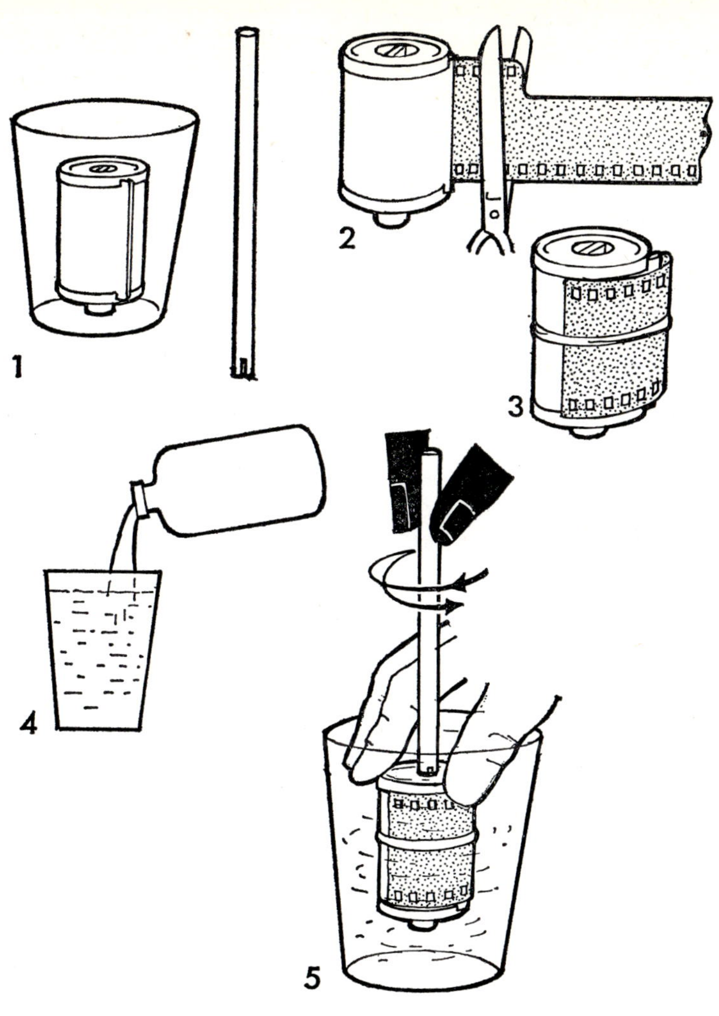

Rapid daylight monobath processing of 35mm film. 1, Equipment required. 2, Trim leader from film. 3, Wrap first two inches of film round cassette and secure with rubber band. 4, Pour monobath into beaker. 5, Lower cassette into beaker while twisting rod to and fro. For fuller details, see page 142.

This procedure involves processing the film in the cassette. The only equipment required is a small beaker or measure, large enough to accommodate sufficient monobath solution to submerge the cassette, and a stirring rod that fits into the cassette spool. The latter can be made from dowel of the appropriate diameter. Rubber or plastic gloves should be worn while carrying out the processing procedure.

The procedure is only suitable for a 20-exposure 35 mm film and requires that two blank exposures are made at the beginning of the film and two at the end, i.e. 16 frames exposed. After exposing the film, the leader must not be wound into the cassette, but must be left protruding. If difficulty is met in leaving the leader protruding from the cassette, it can be attached to the camera take-up spool with adhesive tape when loading the camera. The procedure is as follows:

1 Before submerging the film in the monobath solution, cut off the shaped film leader, fold approximately an inch of film around the cassette and secure with a rubber band.
2 Pour sufficient monobath solution into the measure so that the cassette will become fully submerged.
3 Insert the stirring rod in the cassette spool and rotate clockwise to tighten the film on the spool. Then rotate the rod anti-clockwise whilst counting the number of turns till resistance is felt and the film is unwound. These operations must be carried out carefully and the film must not be wound or unwound too tightly or it may be scratched or kinked.
4 Lower the cassette slowly into the monobath solution while winding and unwinding the film by rotating the rod clockwise and anti-clockwise by the number of turns determined earlier.
5 Carry out the rotating action twice while lowering the cassette into the monobath. When the cassette is fully submerged, continue winding the film for half the number of turns originally found to leave the film at the mid-point of the rotating procedure. Then continue rotating the rod by about 1½ turns in clockwise and anti-clockwise directions throughout the processing time of at least 3½ minutes at 20°C or 68°F or for 2½ minutes at 30°C or 86°F.

6 After the recommended processing time, remove the film from the monobath, allow solution to drain and discard the monobath.
7 Immerse the cassette in water at approximately the same temperature as the monobath solution. Remove the film from the cassette, rinse it for about one minute and hang up to dry

Monobaths can, of course, be used for processing films in normal developing tanks and lead to very short processing times. If complete permanence of the negatives is required, conventional fixing and washing may have to be carried out at a later date, but most commercially available monobaths yield negatives of sufficient permanence for general use.

With monobath processing of a black-and-white negative film, a finished print could be made within approximately half an hour of taking the photograph.

Processing at High Temperatures

Even in the so-called temperate climates, it is not all that rare for temperatures greater than 35°C or 95°F to occur, especially in rooms that are in direct sunshine for much of the day. In tropical climates, temperatures may rise to as high as 49°C or 120°F in the shade. At certain times, high temperatures may also be accompanied by a high relative humidity.

Effects of high temperature

High temperatures and/or high humidities have harmful effects on photographic emulsions and processing solutions. Accordingly, special precautions must be taken when handling and processing photographic materials in these extreme conditions. High humidities and temperatures encourage the growth of moulds and bacterial attack on the gelatin of the film. Also, if films are stored under these conditions before exposing, a high fog level and a loss in film speed will result. After exposure and before processing, latent image fading may occur, and under extreme conditions of humidity and temperature the film may become totally useless.

Processing solutions suffer decomposition if stored at high temperatures for long periods of time (see page 53). Processing at high temperatures will, unless precautions are taken, result in excessive swelling or melting of the emulsion. Swelling of the emulsion makes it more susceptible to mechanical damage and may even cause it to be stripped from the film base.

Reticulation, with resulting degradation in image quality, is likely to occur on transferring a swollen emulsion layer from a solution at a high temperature to a colder solution. Also, swollen gelatin layers contain more absorbed water than unswollen layers and so will take longer to dry. The drying time may be further lengthened under conditions of high humidity, and if conditions are excessively humid the film may never dry completely but remain tacky.

Developing at high temperatures modifies the photographic properties of films, even if correspondingly shorter times are used. The fog level increases and the contrast decreases, neither of which are desirable. Steps must be taken to keep the fog level and contrast within acceptable limits when processing at high temperatures.

Precautions against undesirable effects

Manufacturers sell their films in sealed packets or containers which, if stored unopened, protect the film against high humidities. If kept at high temperatures (48°C or 120°F), even in sealed containers, the life of films may be reduced to weeks. A storage life of six months is the recommended maximum time for black-and-white films kept in their sealed containers at a temperature of 32°C or 90°F. Colour films deteriorate more rapidly than black-and-white films and should be stored in a refrigerator, if possible. When removing the film from cold storage, it must be left at ambient temperature for about half an hour before opening the sealed packet. If the packet is opened when the film is cold, moisture in the air will condense on the film.

After the film has been exposed, it is also subject to deterioration which is aggravated by humidity as the film is no longer in its sealed humidity-proof packet or container. The effects of humidity can be minimised by sealing the film in a container with silica gel as a drying agent as soon as it is removed from the camera. Processing the film as soon as possible after exposure is also recommended.

In tropical conditions, cold storage of photographic films is recommended, together with keeping the film in humidity-proof containers or packets. Temperatures below 16°C or 60°F are preferable.

Processing solutions do not keep at all well at high temperatures. If it is not possible to store them at temperatures below 32°C or 90°F, it is better to buy powdered chemicals rather than concentrated solutions and make them up immediately before processing. For the processing itself, it is best to keep the temperature of the processing solutions at their recommended temperatures by cooling them in cold water or ice baths, in which case no additional precautions are required. For colour processes, this is essential; but as some colour processes are designed for use at relatively high temperatures (e.g. Kodak E-4 process at 30°C), this is not too difficult to achieve by using cooling baths, even if the ambient temperature is above this value.

For black-and-white films, if it is not possible to keep the temperature below 24°C or 75°F, special tropical developers or a pre-hardening bath must be used, together with a stop-hardening bath and an acid-hardening fixing bath.

Tropical developers contain a relatively high concentration of sodium sulphate in addition to the normal developer constituents (see page 64), which reduces the amount of swelling of the emulsion layer at the higher developing temperatures used. They also tend to be less alkaline than developers which are used under normal conditions.

Washing films at high temperatures causes further swelling of the emulsion, but this can be lessened by using stop-hardening and acid-hardening fixing solutions, together with a shortened washing time of about 10–15 minutes. If processing is carried out at a temperature below 24°C or 75°F, but the wash water supply is above this temperature, it is necessary to ensure that the film is adequately hardened by the use of an acid-hardening fixing bath. Washing in changes of water (see page 80) may be advantageously carried out, using water cooled to the same temperature as the processing solutions.

Drying may present problems if high temperatures are accompanied by high humidities and may be aided by an alcohol-water pre-drying bath (see page 141).

Processing at high temperatures

The procedures used for high temperature processing are essentially the same as those used at normal temperatures, except that different solution formulae are used to lessen the effects of temperature on the photographic and mechanical properties of the emulsion. Colour processes are carried out only at the recommended temperature and there is no possibility of processing colour films at elevated temperatures.

Most manufacturers supply specially packaged and formulated processing chemicals for use under tropical conditions for black-and-white negative materials. Processing at high temperatures may involve the use of a pre-hardening bath followed by conventional developing, stop, fixing and washing processes carried out for correspondingly shorter times.

Alternatively, specially formulated solutions may be used which contain constituents that minimise swelling and harden the emulsion so that photographic and mechanical properties of the emulsion are little affected by the high temperatures used.

Processing Black-and-White Prints

In addition to the basic items such as measuring cylinders, bottles, funnels, etc., listed on page 35 for film processing, you will need the following items of equipment for print processing:

1 At least three developing dishes.
2 Two pairs of print forceps.
3 A dish thermometer.
4 A dish warmer.
5 A darkroom clock.
6 A syphon or print washer.
7 A safelight.
8 A print dryer or glazer.

No mention has been made of the choice of enlarger or details of the printing process itself because we are concerned here with the processing operations and not a detailed discussion of enlarging. Items 4, 5, 6 and 8 are not essential and satisfactory prints can be made without them, although a print dryer or glazer is a more convenient and rapid way of drying prints than hanging them up to dry in the air and can give glossy prints when a glossy-surfaced paper is used.

Processing dishes

Print processing is conveniently carried out in dishes which may be constructed of glass, stainless steel or plastics. Properly designed dishes are rectangular in shape with a lip at one corner for ease of pouring out solutions, and generally have a ribbed bottom so that prints do not stick and can easily be lifted out with print forceps. Most dishes also have raised ridges on the underneath surface to aid rocking of the dish during processing so that even agitation can be obtained.

Three such dishes are needed – one for the developer, a second for the stop bath, and the third for the fixer. If a sink syphon or print washer is not used, then a fourth dish is also required for washing prints.

Apart from considerations of cost, the suitability of the constructional material and general design, a decision has to be taken as to the size of the dishes to be bought. For developing, dishes should be approximately one inch larger all round than

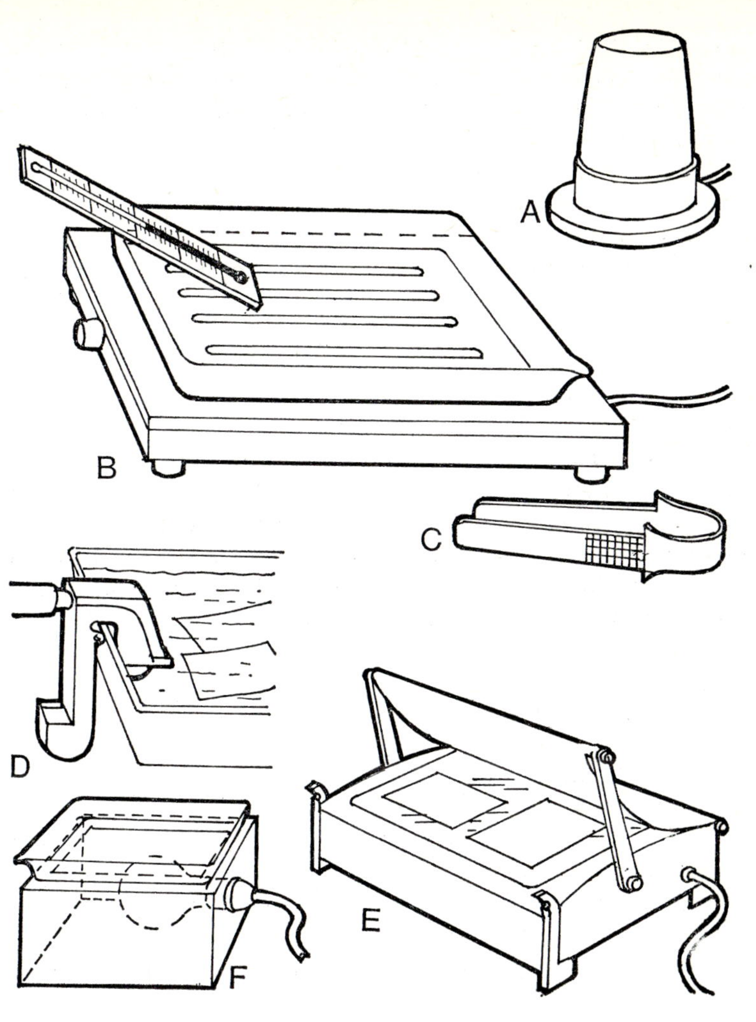

Print processing equipment. **A,** Safelight. **B,** Developing dish, thermometer and heater. **C,** Print tongs. **D,** Syphon print washer. **E,** Dryer and glazer. **F,** Simple dishwarmer

the size of the paper being used. Dishes larger than this use uneconomic quantities of solution. Dishes for fixing and washing can be considerably larger because it is customary to fix and wash a large number of prints at one time. Ideally, all the dishes should be of different colours, so that developer, stop bath and fixer are always used in the corresponding dish to avoid contamination. If dishes of the same colour are used, the dishes should be marked on the outside to indicate the solution with which they are to be used.

Print forceps

Print forceps should always be used for transferring prints from one dish to another to avoid dermatitis and finger marks. For black-and-white print processing, two pairs of print forceps are needed – one to transfer the prints from developer to the stop bath and the other to transfer the prints from the stop bath to the fixer and from the fixer to the wash. To avoid solution contamination, print forceps should be colour coded so that they are used with the appropriate solutions.

Dish thermometers

A dish thermometer is necessary to ensure that the correct processing temperature is used. They are normally made such that they are held in the dish, either by a clip or suction pad, in a convenient position for ease of reaching. They should have clear temperature markings, over an approximate range of 10–40°C or 50–104°F, which are clearly legible under safelight conditions.

Dish warmers

As with film processing, it is necessary to maintain solutions, especially the developer, at the recommended temperature, which is normally within the range 18–24°C or 65–75°F. At lower temperatures processing solutions act more slowly and some not at all, whereas at temperatures greater than 24°C the developer tends to stain the paper.

If the temperature is allowed to fluctuate during processing, or from one processing session to the next processing session, it is impossible to obtain reproducible results. Proprietary dish warmers are available, complete with thermostatic control, but are relatively expensive. Alternatively, a small thermostatically controlled immersion heater may be used. These contain a heating element and a temperature-sensing switch all sealed in a glass tube and are relatively inexpensive.

A simple dish warmer, however, can be constructed by enclosing a 60-watt light bulb in a tin, on which the processing dish is placed. The correct temperature of the solution is maintained by switching the bulb on and off as required. When making such a dish warmer, it is important to make sure that it is light-tight and that electrical connections are properly earthed and are waterproof.

Darkroom clocks

Although satisfactory prints can be made without accurately timing development, by developing to completion for about three minutes, the time of development affects the results and too short a development time produces flat prints with a low maximum density, while excessive development is likely to result in stained or foggy prints. It is better darkroom practice to carry out print development for the recommended time. Accordingly, you would be wise to obtain a darkroom clock with a large luminous dial and a large sweep second hand for accurately timing the short development periods used in print processing.

Syphons and print washers

The easiest way of washing prints is to use a simple syphon fixed to the sink waste pipe, while ensuring thorough agitation of prints in the sink by directing a stream of water below the surface with a rubber tube attached to the tap. The syphon may be constructed from PVC tubing in appropriate diameters and a rubber plug or bung, or may be bought at modest cost. Inexpensive syphons are also available which clip to the sides of processing dishes. They direct a stream of water into the dish with sufficient force to agitate the prints vigorously and at the same time automatically discharge the wash water. Various types of automatic print washer are currently available which wash prints in continuous changes of water while maintaining vigorous agitation of the prints.

Safelights

Some typical types of safelight suitable for amateur use are shown on page 32. These are provided with suitable safelight filters for black-and-white print processing and some have interchangeable filters so that they can also be used as safelights for colour-print processing. They emit orange or yellow-green light and are bright enough for easy working.

Print dryers and glazers

A flat-bed dryer or glazer is the simplest type of device available for rapidly drying prints by heat. When used with a chromium-plated glazing sheet, to which prints are squeegeed face downwards, glossy prints are obtained when 'glossy surface' printing papers are used. These are very convenient for drying prints made on conventional photographic papers but must not be used for drying resin-coated papers. Resin-coated papers are best dried by removing excess water with a sponge or print-wiper then hanging them up or holding them in front of a fan heater or hair dryer. Although purpose-made dryers are available for these papers as a rather expensive alternative. Both types of prints may be air-dried by laying them on blotting paper or on home-made racks covered with a fine curtain mesh.

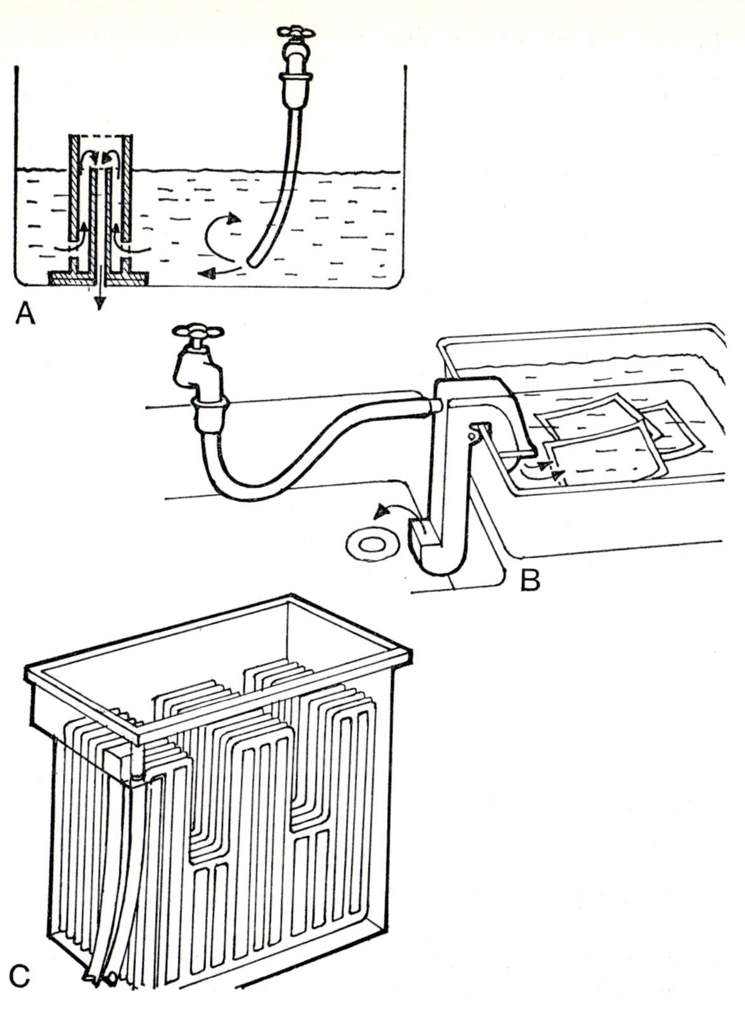

Print washing equipment. **A,** Sink syphon. **B,** Dish syphon. **C,** 'Toast-rack' print washer

Processing procedure

Developing black-and-white prints is an analogous process to film processing in which the invisible latent image formed by exposure of the paper to the negative in the enlarger or contact printer is made visible. It is the most interesting and fascinating of all photographic processes so far described because the image is seen to appear during development. Safelights are sufficiently bright to observe the process. The sequence of operations is much the same as for black-and-white negatives and involves stages of development, stopping development by a stop bath, fixing, followed by washing and drying. The main difference is that processing is carried out in open dishes or trays in a darkroom illuminated by a safelight. Approximate times for a typical processing sequence are given in the table below.

BLACK-AND-WHITE PRINT PROCESSING

Stage	Approximate time at 20°C or 68°F	
	Conventionial Paper	Resin-coated Paper
1. Development	1–3 min	35–60 sec
2. Stop bath	5–10 sec	5–10 sec
3. Fixation	5–10 min	30 sec
4. Wash	30–60 min	30–120 sec
5. Dry	?	10–15 min. (room temp)*

*Glossy RC materials dry to a high gloss without glazing.

Print development

Print developers contain similar ingredients to those indicated for use in black-and-white film developers on page 64, but are generally formulated somewhat differently because they are usually required to give blue-black images with emulsions of different composition and are used in open dishes.

During development, the image is seen to appear and there is a tendency with many workers to judge the appearance of the print and remove it from the developer when it appears to have reached sufficient density and contrast. There are various reasons why this is bad practice and development for a constant

time should always be carried out. First, safelights are inadequate in terms of intensity and colour for judging print quality. Secondly, it is the exposure in the enlarger that should be used to control the density of the print. With an under-exposed print and an excessively long development time used in an attempt to obtain sufficient density, staining and/or fogging of the print is likely. With an over-exposed print and under-development, results are likely to be of too low contrast and may be mottled or uneven, owing to insufficient development. Slight variations in development time are permissible to compensate for *slight* under or over-exposure of the prints. Finally, the appearance of the print changes when it is fixed. This can be misleading because the unexposed and un-developed silver halides give a veiling effect which is removed by fixing. So for consistent results always develop prints for the recommended time and alter the density of the print by the exposure.
Print developer, like any developer, becomes exhausted with use. A check must be made of the number and sizes of prints developed, and either the developer discarded when the specified number or area has been put through or the developer should be replenished according to the manufacturer's recommendations.

Stop bath

Immediately following development, the print is transferred to the stop bath in order to arrest development, minimise risk of staining and to prolong the life of the fixer. Some print stop baths contain an indicator which changes colour when the bath is exhausted. This eliminates the need for guesswork or calculation of the number of prints put through, in deciding whether the bath is still active.

Fixation

After development has been stopped, fixing is the next step to be undertaken. This is normally carried out in a conventional fixer of the acid-hardening type (see page 76). In print fixing, it is especially important not to fix the prints for a longer time than is recommended. Excessive time of immersion in a fixing bath is likely to cause image degradation in two ways. The image tone may change and the image may begin to bleach out with resulting loss in highlight detail. Also, substantial amounts of hypo are absorbed by the paper base and cannot be removed within the normal washing time. The result is stained or faded images on storage or if drying by heat is used.

Generally, a fixing time of 5–10 minutes is recommended as being adequate for conventional papers in a single fixing bath. Surprisingly, it is more economic and efficient to use two fixing baths, approximately five minutes in each. In two-bath fixation, the first bath does most of the fixing by removing the majority of the unexposed silver halides, while the second bath remains relatively fresh. When the first bath is exhausted (worked out from the supplier's data and the total area put through), it is discarded and replaced by the second bath, and a fresh solution replaces the second fixing bath. This cycle may be repeated for about 4–5 times before starting again with two fresh solutions. When two-bath fixation is used, it has been shown that for a given quantity of fixer twice the number of prints may be fixed than when a single bath is used. For resin-coated papers a fixing time of around 30 seconds is usually sufficient.

Washing and drying

When fixing has been completed, the prints are transferred to a suitable washing device such as those shown on page 159, in which it is important to make sure that the prints do not stick to one another and that they are thoroughly agitated. Periodically turning the prints over by hand insures against prints sticking together and being incompletely washed. After the recommended washing time and removal of the prints from the washer, excess water should be wiped from the prints and the prints hung up to dry or dried by placing them face down on a sheet of photographic-grade blotting paper. Alternatively, they can be dried by heat (see page 158).

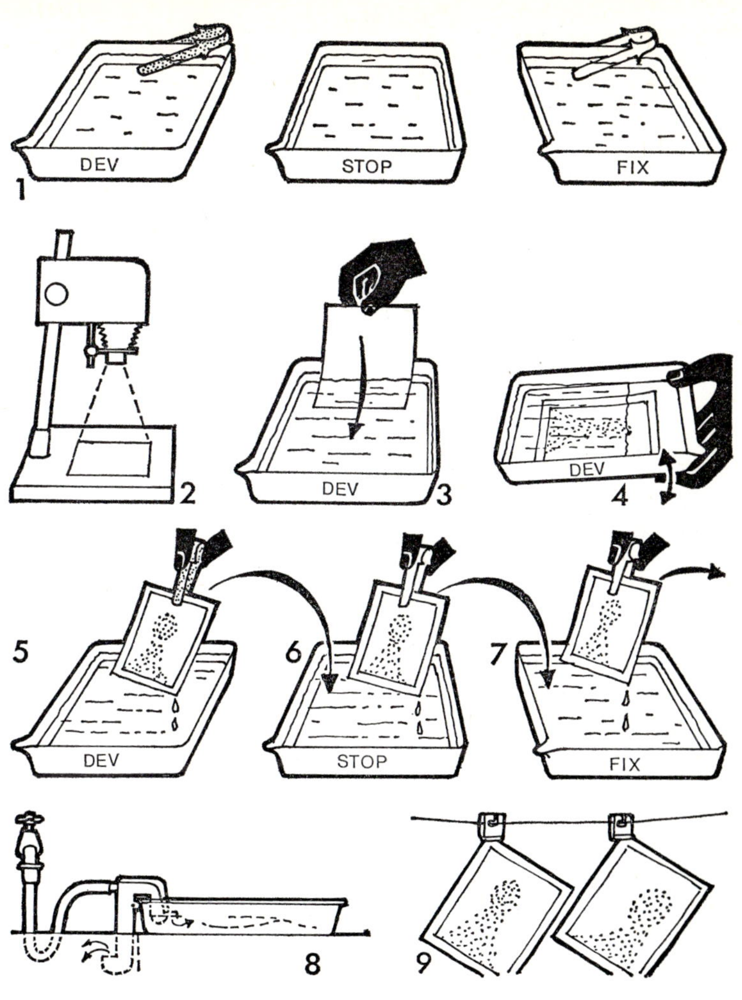

Processing black and white prints. 1, Lay out solutions in correct sequence. 2, Expose paper. 3, Place paper in developer. 4, Agitate continuously. 5, Drain print and transfer to stop bath. 6, Drain print and transfer to fixer. 7, Drain print and transfer to wash. 8, Wash. 9, Dry.

Practical print processing

Before beginning a printing and processing session, it is necessary to prepare the solutions and make sure that they are at the recommended working temperature. The techniques for the preparation and dilution of solutions are exactly the same as those given on pages 46 to 52. When the solutions are ready, proceed as follows:

1 Pour the solutions into the processing dishes and place the dishes in the sequence used for processing – develop – stop – fix.
2 Turn off the darkroom light, switch on the safelight, and expose the paper.
3 After the paper has been exposed, remove it from the enlarger or contact printer and place it in the developer. To do this, grasp it firmly by the edges and slide it quickly and evenly, emulsion side upward, into the developer, making sure that the developer covers the whole print. Rock the tray gently. If the print should curl up out of the developer, push it down with the print forceps. With thin papers it may be convenient to place them initially in the developer emulsion side downward and then turn them emulsion side up with the print forceps.
4 Continue rocking the dish gently during the whole of the development time.
5 A few seconds before the end of the recommended developing time, lift the print out of the developer, using the print forceps, and allow to drain. Then transfer to the stop bath. taking care not to dip the developer forceps in the stop bath
6 Continually rock the stop bath dish for 5–10 seconds, then pick the print up by the edges, using the *second* pair of print forceps, allow to drain and transfer to fixer.
7 Agitate the print vigorously in the fixer for one to two minutes before turning the light on. Thereafter, agitate occasionally until fixing has been carried out for the recommended time. During the printing session, a number of prints will build up in the fixer. For satisfactory fixing, do not allow the prints to lie in contact with one another, but make sure that their positions are changed and the solution

is agitated so that the fixing solution can reach the print surface.

8 When fixing is complete, allow the prints to drain for a few seconds and transfer them to the wash, and wash them for at least 30 minutes with thorough agitation.

9 After completion of the washing cycle, remove the prints from the wash water, allow them to drain, wipe off surface water, and dry.

When your printing and processing session is over, do not forget to discard exhausted solutions; return other solutions to their bottles and rinse the dishes thoroughly before drying them and putting them away.

The times given in the text refer to conventionial photographic papers but these times have been reduced substantially by the introduction of resin-coated paper and the appropriate processing chemicals (see table on page 160). The main advantages of these papers are that the washing and drying stages are far more rapid than conventionial papers because the paper onto which the emulsion is coated is "sealed" on both surfaces by a coating of polythene for example, which prevents the paper fibres from absorbing processing chemicals and water. The processing is speeded up further by the use of more active developer and fixer solutions.

Processing Colour Prints

Practically all manufacturers who market colour paper also sell the appropriate processing kit, together with instructions for its use. There are also independent suppliers of photographic products and chemicals who, while not manufacturing colour paper, do supply chemical kits for processing some of the available makes of colour paper.

The whole area of colour paper and its processing is a branch of photographic technology which, at the present time, is changing quite rapidly. Currently available processes are likely to be superseded by simpler processes which require fewer processing solutions. Colour papers are of the resin-coated type which requires no glazing, but rapidly dries to a highly glossy surface. Kodak RC type papers are typical examples and are also available with other surfaces.

The papers and processes listed below are examples of widely used materials suitable for home-processing. This list is a guide and is not meant to be exhaustive because processes are being simplified, modified and generally improved. For the latest details, you would be well advised to consult your photographic dealer to find out the availability of the papers and processes listed.

COLOUR PRINT MATERIALS FOR HOME PROCESSING

Paper	Process
(a) For Prints from negatives	
Agfacolor MCN 310/312/317 Type 4/PE	Agfacolor Process 85
Agfacolor MCN 310/312/317 Type 5/PE	Agfacolor Process P
Kodak Ektacolor 74 RC	Ektaprint 3 or 2
Unicolor RB	Unicolor, Total Color
(b) For Prints from slides	
Cibachrome-A	Cibachrome-A P-12
Kodak Ektachrome RC Type 1993	Ektaprint R500
Kodak Ektachrome 14 RC	Ektaprint R14
Kodak Ektachrome RC Type 2203 (available in US)	Ektaprint R100

Some of the processes listed are available only in 'Professional Packs' which may make five or more litres of each solution. These quantities will very likely be far more than you are likely to need and with some processes the packs cannot be divided to make up smaller volumes of solutions.

I am sure that a reputable dealer in photographic materials will be in the best position to advise you on the suitability and availability of colour-print processing kits for home-processing when you feel ready to embark on this aspect of processing.

Storage of colour paper

Colour paper is best stored in its sealed packet in a refrigerator at a temperature not exceeding 10°C or 30°F. Colour papers are protected by moisture-proof packets which, after opening, are liable to change in their printing characteristics due to the effects of heat and humidity. Accordingly, it is better to buy papers in packets containing just sufficient quantities for each processing and printing session. Before opening the packet, it should be allowed to warm up to room temperature if it was stored in a refrigerator before use, in order to avoid condensation.

Special equipment

The basic equipment and techniques used for black-and-white print processing (see page 154) are also suitable for colour-print processing, with one or two minor changes.

An appropriate safelight is necessary. This is usually amber or dark green in colour and gives a very low level of illumination which makes dish processing more difficult for colour papers than for black-and-white papers. Dish processing, however, can be done away with altogether to avoid the difficulty of manipulation in an almost totally black darkroom, by using simple and inexpensive processing drums or daylight developing tanks (see page 170).

Like colour-film processing, colour-print processing requires strict temperature control ($\pm\frac{1}{4}$°C for development) and a thermostatically controlled dish warmer of the type described on page 156 is desirable if dish processing is to be used.

Colour-print processing sometimes involves more processing steps than are used in black-and-white print processing, although two solution processes are now readily available. For dish processing, up to four dishes of the appropriate size may be required.

Daylight colour-print processors

Instead of using a number of dishes and transferring the paper from dish to dish, a drum processor or daylight developing tank may be used advantageously. Daylight colour-print processing devices suitable for the home processor are, in general, no more expensive than the four or so processing dishes which would otherwise be used. They are used in much the same way as daylight developing tanks, which, after loading in the darkroom, processing solutions are poured in in the correct sequence under white light conditions.

Daylight colour-print processors offer a number of advantages when compared with dish processing:

1 Only one drum is required.

2 After loading in the darkroom, all further processing operations are carried out in white light.

3 Accurate temperature control can be achieved without using expensive dish warmers or thermostatic heaters.

4 Excellent reproducibility of results is obtained as one-shot processing is used.

5 Only small volumes of processing solutions are needed.

6 Agitation is very easily carried out.

7 There is little likelihood of the developer or other processing solutions coming into contact with your hands.

There are many examples of daylight colour print processors which have many features in common but differ in their design and mode of use. The significant features common to all processing drums may be summarized as follows:

1 They are loaded in the darkroom with the back surface of the paper in contact with the drum and the emulsion surface towards the centre.

2 All are provided with a means of introducing solutions and draining them from the drum in the light.

3 Only small volumes of processing solutions are needed (50–90 ml per 8 × 10 inch print).

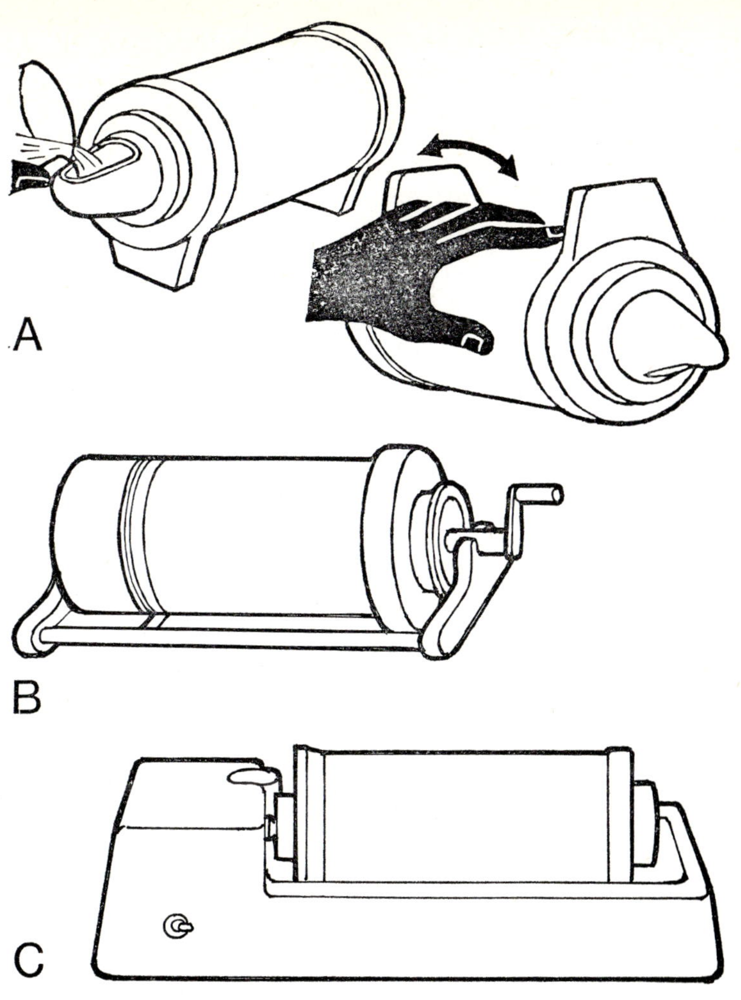

Three colour processing drums with three different methods of agitation. A, Simma color drum, manual rolling (motorized agitatior is also available). B, Paterson Colour Print Processor with cradle and hand crank. C, Jobo Color Processor with automatic rolling and constant temperature bath.

4 Processing chemicals only come into contact with the emulsion surface when the drum is rolled in the horizontal position.
5 Agitation is carried out by rolling the drums.

The most common size appropriate to the needs of the home processor is a drum for processing one 8 × 10 inch print although larger drums are available.

The main differences between drums of different manufacture may be summarized as follows:

1 The way in which solutions are introduced and kept separate from the print until processing starts.
2 The recommended means of temperature control.
3 The type and method of agitation.
4 The way in which solutions are drained from the drum.

Colour print processing drums may be divided into two basic types. First there are those in which solutions are introduced with the drum in the vertical position and second there are those in which solutions are introduced with the drum in the horizontal position.

The types of drum with vertical introduction of solution (e.g. Cibachrome, Durst Codrum) keep the solution separate from the paper by holding the liquid in a small 'cup' fixed to the underside of the lid immediately below the filling hole. The solution only flows from the 'cup' into the main body of the drum when it is tilted to the horizontal position, so allowing the solution to flow through slots around the top of the 'cup'. However in the Kodak Printank solutions enter the main body of the drum via a tube which leads the solution to the bottom of the drum below the paper. On tilting the drum the solution flows over the surface of the paper.

Those drums with horizontal introduction of solution (e.g. Beseler, Simmacolor, Unicolor, etc.) keep the solution separate from the paper surface either by a small trough running along the length of the drum fixed to the end-cap, or by a trough formed at the bottom of the drum between the guides that hold the paper in position. By rolling the drum the solution is allowed to flow over the surface of the print. Processing of colour prints in all currently available drums usually requires a pre-wash before development. This serves two purposes.

Firstly it ensures even development by the small volume of developer used. Secondly it is used as a means of temperature control. For temperature control by this method water, usually at a higher temperature than both room temperature and the process temperature, is used. The required temperature for the pre-wash is found from charts or calculators provided with the processing drum. This method of temperature control requires that the temperature of the room in which processing is carried out be known. Some drums use a thermostatic water bath in which the drum is mechanically rotated as a means of temperature control whilst many manufacturers of drums offer a motorized drive stand for automatic agitation. These do tend to be relatively expensive. Manual agitation by rolling the drum on a flat surface is an effective method although somewhat tedious. To ensure efficient agitation some drums use a 'wave-wash' or 'rock and roll' method which is effected by eccentric flanges around the drum so that as it is rolled on a flat surface it also goes up and down.

Processing steps

Processing of colour prints is analogous to colour-negative processing and essentially similar solutions are used.

Warning notes about possible harmful effects of colour processing solutions are always provided by the manufacturer of the processing kit and should be very carefully studied before using the chemicals.

A typical sequence for colour print processing is given below for the Ektaprint 3 processing of Kodak 74 RC papers.

1 Colour develop.
2 Bleach-fix.
3 Wash.
4 Stabilize.
5 Dry.

This process involves only three processing solutions and takes eight minutes at 31°C or 88°F. An additional advantage of using this paper is that it requires no glazing, but is rapidly dried at a temperature of 80–85°C or 176–185°F to a glossy surface.

Agfa and similar types of processing chemicals also use bleach-fix solutions, and their existing processing procedures are relatively simple, involving up to four solutions. A typical processing sequence of the Agfa type is as follows:

1 Colour develop.
2 Stop.
3 Wash.
4 Bleach-fix.
5 Wash.
6 Stabilize.
7 Dry.

Typical processing times of 18 minutes are obtained at a temperature of up to 30°C or 86°F. A shorter process of about 9 minutes at 42°C is also available and recommended by Agfa for the home processer.

All the above procedures are those used for processing prints obtained from colour negatives. In addition to these procedures there are special papers, chemicals and procedures for obtaining a print from a colour transparency. This may be accomplished by printing the transparency on a reversal paper, which is then processed by a reversal processing procedure to yield a positive print. The processing operations parallel those for the reversal processing of colour reversal films (page 25). A typical example of a reversal paper and process is Kodak Ektachrome 14 RC Reversal Paper in Ektaprint R 14 chemicals.

Like processing of colour reversal films, colour reversal paper requires the following steps:

1 First or black-and-white develop.
2 Stop.
3 Wash.
4 Reversal exposure.
5 Colour develop.
6 Wash.
7 Bleach-fix.
8 Wash.
9 Stabilize.
10 Dry.

An alternative and very popular method for obtaining prints from slides is by the Cibachrome method. The principles of this method are quite different from any of the colour materials that we have considered. Instead of forming dyes during colour development the dyes (cyan, magenta and yellow) are already present in the coated material in the form of an integral tripack. These are bleached in image-wise manner during processing to give a direct positive print. The bleach solution is of a totally different chemical composition to any of the bleaches used in the more usual colour processes and is very acidic. Another difference is that the sensitive layers are not coated onto paper which could not withstand the acidic bleach solution but is coated on a pigmented film base that is very like paper in its appearance.

The processing of Cibachrome material is far simpler than processing of reversal papers, involving fewer stages. In addition the temperature tolerance during processing is much greater ($\pm 1\frac{1}{2}$°C). The processing sequence is as follows:

1 Develop.
2 Bleach.
3 Fix.
4 Wash.

The total time for Cibachrome-A is 12 minutes at 24°C for the Cibachrome P-12 process.

Cibachrome materials have certain advantages when compared with other colour photographic materials. The dyes used are very stable to light and fade far less readily. Images are sharper and more brilliant because the dyes act as filters during exposure and prevent the 'spreading' of light by scattering and reflection. Processing is short and involves fewer solutions than are needed for reversal papers.

The main disadvantage from the user's point of view is that the bleach solution is very acidic and must be treated with extreme caution. The processing kits are provided with a neutralizer solution which must be mixed with the bleach before it can be discarded.

More exact details of this process and the previously described processes can be found in the tables on pages 176 to 179, which contain times, temperatures, etc., for specific processes.

Whatever processing chemicals and paper you finally adopt, the manufacturers' recommendations must be carefully followed and no attempt whatsoever should be made to interchange processing solutions from one process to another. As for all photographic processing procedures, and especially for colour processing, contamination must be completely avoided.
Colour prints should be dried by one of the techniques given on page 158 for resin-coated papers.

Summary of procedures

The following tables summarize the steps involved in the processing of various colour papers. All times are total times for each stage and include the draining time for the processor used. If a drum or tube processor is used, a pre-soak is required, details for which are supplied with the processing device.

AGFACOLOR MCN 310/312/317 TYPE 4 IN PROCESS 85 CHEMICALS

Stage	20°C Time (min)	20°C Temp (°C)	25°C Time (min)	25°C Temp (°C)	30°C Time (min)	30°C Temp (°C)
1. Pre-wash*	1	**	1	**	1	**
2. Colour develop	10	20±0·5	5	25±0·3	3	30±0·3
3. Stop	2	15–25	1–2	15–25	1–2	25–30
4. Wash	2	15–25	1–2	15–25	1–2	15–30
5. Bleach-fix	6	20±1	5	25±1	4	30±1
6. Wash	6	15–25	6	15–25	4	15–30
7. Stabilize	2	15–25	2	15–25	2	15–30
8. Dry	—	—	—	—	—	—
Total time (excluding drying)	29 minutes		23 minutes		18 minutes	

* If processing in dishes omit the pre-wash.

** Use the pre-wash temperature recommended in the instructions provided with the drum.

AGFACOLOR MCN 310/312/317 TYPE 4 HIGH TEMPERATURE PROCESS IN PROCESS 85 CHEMICALS

Stage	Time (min)	Temp (°C)
1. Pre-wash	1	**
2. Colour develop	1¾	42±0·3
3. Stop	½	42
4. Wash	½	42
5. Bleach–fix	2½	42
6. Wash	3×½	42
7. Stabilize	1	42
8. Dry	—	—
Total time (excluding drying)	9¼ minutes	

KODAK EKTACOLOR 74 RC PAPER IN EKTAPRINT 3 CHEMICALS

Stage	Time (min)	Temp (°C)
1. Pre-wash	1	**
2. Colour develop	3½	31±0·25
3. Bleach–fix	1½	31±1
4 Wash	2	31±1
5. Stabilize	1	31±1
6. Dry	—	< 85
Total time (excluding drying)	8 minutes	

**Use the pre-wash temperature recommended in the instructions provided with the drum.

KODAK EKTACOLOR 74 RC IN ALTERNATIVE CHEMICALS

Stage	Photocolor II** Time (min)	Temp (°C)	Unicolor Total Color** Time (min)	Temp (°C)
1. Pre-wash	1	*	1	*
2. Colour develop	2	38	2	40
3. Stop	¼	38	¼	40
4. Bleach-fix	1	38	1	40
5. Wash	2	34–38	1	40
6. Stabilize	–	—	½	20–40
7. Dry	–	85	—	85
Total time (excluding drying)	6¼ minutes		5¾ minutes	

KODAK EKTACHROME RC TYPE 1993 REVERSAL PAPER IN R–500 CHEMICALS

Stage	Time (min)	Temp (°C)
1. Pre-wash	1	*
2. First develop	1½	38±0·3
3. Stop	½	38±0·6
4. Wash	2	38±1·1
5. Colour develop	3	38±0·6
6. Wash	½	38±1·1
7. Bleach–fix	1½	38±0·6
8. Wash	1½	38±1·1
9. Stabilize	1	38±0·6
10. Rinse	¼	38±1·1
11. Dry	—	49–66
Total time (excluding drying	12¾ minutes	

* Use the pre-wash temperature recommended in the instructions provided with the drum.

** The same basic chemicals are used for processing colour negatives and prints, but for prints a special developer additive or different dilution may be required. Full details are provided with the chemicals.

KODAK EKTACHROME 14 RC REVERSAL PAPER IN EKTAPRINT R 14 CHEMICALS

Stage	Time (min)	Temp (°C)
1. Pre-wash	4	*
2. First develop	3	30±0·3
3. Stop	1½	30±1
4. Wash	3	28–35
5. Re-expose	¼	—
6. Colour develop	3¼	30±0·3
7. Wash	1½	28–35
8. Bleach–fix	3	30±1
9. Wash	3¼	28–35
10. Stabilize	1½	30±1
11. Rinse	¼	—
12. Dry	—	< 88
Total time (excluding drying)	24½ minutes	

* Use the pre-wash temperature recommended in the instructions provided with the drum.

CIBACHROME-A IN CIBACHROME P-12 CHEMICALS

	20°C		24°C*		28°C	
Stage	Time (min)	Temp (°C)	Time (min)	Temp (°C)	Time (min)	Temp (°C)
1. Develop	2½	20±1·5	2	24±1·5	1½	28±1·5
2. Bleach	4½	20±1·5	4	24±1·5	3½	28±1·5
3. Fix	3½	20±1·5	3	24±1·5	2½	28±1·5
4. Wash	3	20–24	3	20–24	3	20–24
5. Dry	—	—	—	—	—	—
Total time (excluding drying)	13½ minutes		12 minutes		10½ minutes	

* The recommended processing temperature is 24°C.

** Caution corrosive acidic solution. Always mix with neutralizer before discarding.

Processing Faults

Even the most careful home-processor will, on occasions, produce results that are unsatisfactory. Most faults that are encountered are due to errors in technique which, once the cause has been found, can be corrected. The main purpose of listing such faults is to correct any errors in technique that may be made.

It is extremely rare for manufacturers to supply faulty material, and any faults obtained are almost certainly due to errors in camera exposure, solution mixing or processing, all of which can be avoided once their cause has been found.

Fault analysis

In order to establish the causes of errors, films should be inspected in:

1 The image as a whole.
2 The shadow areas.
3 The highlight areas.
4 The margins or borders.

The image as a whole may appear too light or too dark or, for colour processes, one colour may predominate. If on a whole roll of film only a few frames have these defects, the most likely cause of error is in the camera exposure. If, on the other hand, the complete roll of film shows these defects on every frame, the errors are more likely to be in the processing technique and were probably caused by under or over-development.

The image should also be inspected for evenness, staining and random spots or markings, which, if present, will most probably have been caused by processing errors.

The shadow areas should be almost transparent in negatives, but still show some detail, whereas in positives or transparencies they should be almost as dense as the margins and, in a colour transparency, may appear slightly blue. If there is density in the shadows of a negative, but no apparent detail, it is likely that fogging has occurred. Transparencies should appear dense and neutral in the shadow areas, but contain some detail.

The highlights in negatives should have a moderately high density. If the density is low, under-development, under-exposure, or both are possible causes. In transparencies, the highlights should be almost transparent, with no objectionable colour bias. If the highlights of a transparency are veiled, incomplete first development or solution contamination are probable causes.

The margins in negative films should be almost transparent, but may show a slight tint, depending on the particular type of film. Colour negative films will have margins that are a uniform orange colour. If the margins appear very dense, this is most likely due to fogging caused either by light or gross over-development.

In reversal films, the margins should appear a uniform high density black. Pale margins may be caused by fogging, inadequate reversal exposure, excessive first development or incomplete second or colour development.

Development faults

Of all the processing errors, over or under-development are the most likely to be encountered. This applies to development of colour and black-and-white negative films as well as the two development stages used for reversal films. Development is the most critical of the stages and developers are the least stable of the processing solutions used. Small changes in the development process or the developer solution are likely to have a great effect on the images that are obtained. If under-development is found to be the source of error, your technique should be investigated for:

1 Developer storage conditions. Was your developer stored for too long or under adverse conditions? Did you allow aerial oxidation of the developer to occur by careless preparation or pouring of solutions?
2 Developer exhaustion. Was the developer used for developing more than the recommended number of films?
3 Dilution. Was the developer diluted correctly?

4 Agitation. Was sufficient agitation given during development?
5 Temperature. Was the correct temperature maintained during development or was it allowed to fall below the recommended value?
6 Time. Was development carried out for the correct time or was too short a time used?

Under-development is caused by all the above factors, and over-development is caused by the converse of items 3 to 6 – i.e. by too concentrated a developer, too much agitation, too high a temperature or too long a development time.

General processing faults

In order to find the causes of processing faults, the accompanying tables list faults according to the principal fault, subsidiary faults and their likely causes. The tables have been divided into seven categories for ease of reference:

1 General faults common to all processes.
2 Faults in black-and-white negative processing.
3 Faults in colour-negative processing.
4 Faults in black-and-white reversal processing.
5 Faults in colour-reversal processing.
6 Faults in black-and-white print processing.
7 Faults in colour-print processing.

GENERAL FAULTS COMMON TO ALL PROCESSES

Principal fault	Subsidiary faults	Possible causes
Lines, scratches	May appear light or dark	Abrasion in camera
	Transparent	Abrasion during washing
Irregular spots	Less dense than surroundings (in negatives)	Air bubbles in developer
	White deposit on film surface	Uneven drying, hard water, or water splashes after drying
	With well defined edges, black or white	Chemical dust on film, dust or scum in solutions Particles in wash water
	Pinholes	Dust in camera
Staining	Local or general	Contamination, exhausted solutions
Uneven density	Patchy appearance	Poor agitation
	Streaks from edges tailing off towards the centre	Light fogging from loosely wound film
Emulsion coming off support at edges (frilling)		Solutions at too high a temperature Wash water too high a temperature, insufficient hardening
Grainy appearance	Wrinkled surface (reticulation)	Sudden temperature change Insufficient hardening
Melting	Irregular deformation	Drying at too high a temperature

FAULTS IN BLACK-AND-WHITE NEGATIVE PROCESSES

Principal fault	Subsidiary faults	Possible causes
Image lacks density	No shadow detail, only highlights recorded	Under-exposure
	Shadow detail present but highlights lack density (contrast low)	Under-development
Image too dense	Good shadow detail, poor highlight detail, edges clear (low contrast)	Over-exposure
Image too dense	Partial reversal	Extreme over-exposure (solarization) or light fogging during development
	Fogged or veiled shadows, dense highlights	Over-exposure and over-development
Fog	Grey or black fog all over including the edges	Gross over-development or Exposure to light
	Edge fog only	Roll film wound too loosely
	Local or general yellowish brown in colour	Exhausted developer
	Dichroic, i.e. appears red by transmitted light and yellow/green by reflected light	Exhausted developers, contamination of developer with fixer Exhausted developer or contaminated fixer Negative exposed to light before fixing complete
Milky appearance		Incomplete fixing

FAULTS IN BLACK-AND-WHITE REVERSAL PROCESSING

Principal fault	Subsidiary faults	Possible causes
Image lacks density	No highlight detail, transparent	Over-exposure, or first development excessive, or second development too short
Image too dense	Dense highlights	Under-exposure or under-first development
Fog	Transparent areas	Film exposed to light before processing
Stain	Local or general yellow or brown	Solutions and/or procedure inappropriate for film

FAULTS IN COLOUR NEGATIVE PROCESSING

Principal fault	Subsidiary faults	Possible causes
Image lacks density	No shadow detail, highlights pale in colour	Under-exposure
	Shadow detail present, highlights pale in colour	Under-development
Image too dense	Reddish edges	Developer contaminated with fixer
	Good shadow detail, poor highlight detail	Over-exposure
	Fogging in shadows, high contrast	Over-development
	Completely opaque	Bleach or fixer omitted
Stain	General, orange in colour	Normal
	Local or general cloudy grey	Incomplete bleaching and/or incomplete fixing
	Bluish spots	Bleach contaminated with iron

FAULTS IN COLOUR REVERSAL PROCESSING

Principal fault	Subsidiary faults	Possible causes
Image lacks density	Overall paleness, margins normal	Over-exposure, excessive first development
	Overall paleness including margins	Insufficient re-exposure or colour development
	Overall paleness and colour cast	First stop bath exhausted Developer contamination
	Overall paleness, margins lack density	Film fogged before processing
	Low maximum density and colour not neutral Margins lack density	Contamination of colour developer with fixer, or colour developer exhausted or oxidized
Image too dense	Overall	Under-exposure, incomplete bleaching or fixing, under-developed in first developer Excessive pre-hardening
Stained highlights	Pink	Contamination of solutions
	Brownish	Incomplete bleaching or fixing
Orange-yellow image		Daylight film exposed to artificial light
Blue image		Artificial light film used and exposed to daylight

Principal fault	Subsidiary faults	Possible causes
Image lacks density	Contrast low	Incorrect choice of paper grade: print over-exposed and under-developed: under development
	Contrast acceptable	Print under-exposed, under-development
Image too dense	Insufficient detail in highlights, dense shadows	Incorrect choice of paper grade
	Highlights veiled	Print over-exposed Over-development
Fog	General fog over whole of print including the borders	Stale paper, safe-light incorrect, gross over-development, fogging by light
Uneven density	Sharp boundaries	Uneven development
	Mottled appearance	Stale paper Exhausted developer
Stain	Yellow-brown over whole print	Incomplete fixing, fixer exhausted, stop-bath exhausted, insufficient time in stop bath, contamination of developer with fixer, fixer contaminated with developer
	Print turns yellow-brown on keeping	Insufficiently fixed Insufficiently washed
Spots	Black with sharp edges	Particles in the developer Air bubbles in fixing bath or stop bath
	White with sharp edges	Air bubbles in the developer Dust in the enlarger

FAULTS IN COLOUR PRINT PROCESSING

Principal fault	Subsidiary faults	Possible causes
Image lacks density		Under-exposure, under-development
	Flat print lacking contrast May have stained highlights	Under-development Exhausted developer
Image too dense		Over-exposure, over-development
Stain	In highlights and borders	Exhausted or stale developer, over-development Contamination of developer by stop-fix or bleach-fix Contamination of bleach or bleach-fix by developer
	In highlights only	Over-exposure and/or under-development
Overall colour cast	Any colour, but white borders	Filtration during printing incorrect
Mottle		Contaminated or exhausted solution. Solution splashing
	Red or blue spots	Iron contamination of wash water
Partial discoloration		Bleach, fix or bleach-fix exhausted or time of treatment too short Drying by excessive heat

NOTE
A great many things can go wrong with colour print processing and the exact nature of particular faults depends upon the individual paper and processing chemicals being used. This table lists only the more common general faults whilst details of the causes of faults in specific processes are generally provided by the colour paper and/or processing kit manufacturer.

Avoiding processing faults

Processing faults unfortunately will occur from time to time, but if systematic and correct procedures are adopted the chances of making a mistake are reduced considerably. Errors caused by contamination of solutions are due to careless work and can be avoided quite easily, as can errors in temperature control and timing.

Other general faults listed in the table on page 185 can be avoided by taking appropriate precautions. For example, if there are small spots on your negative caused by chemical dust or particles in the wash water, these can be avoided by filtering solutions and by fitting a proprietary filter to the tap providing the water for washing your films. If the techniques described in earlier chapters are carefully followed in conjunction with the manufacturer's specific recommendations, faults due to uneven development, drying marks, reticulation, etc., should not occur. The purpose of listing the major processing faults is to find the causes for these errors so that they can be avoided the next time processing is carried out. The purpose is not to give recommendations for 'magical' formulae which can convert a badly processed film into a perfect film. Only in black-and-white processing is some correction to the final image possible by using *intensifiers* and *reducers* which are provided by some manufacturers.

Intensifiers may be used for increasing the density and sometimes contrast of a negative that lacks density, provided that the negative has some perceptible detail in the shadows. They cannot, of course, create an image where none existed.

Reducers are used for reducing the density (and sometimes contrast) of images that are too dense. For example, a transparency with blocked-in highlights could be treated with a reducer to clear the highlights. Similarly, an over-exposed or over-developed negative might be improved by using a reducer. At best, these techniques are risky procedures and there is a distinct chance that the negative will be completely ruined. They should be used as a last resort. For black-and-white negatives, moderate errors in exposure or development are not as serious as they once were, because today there exists a wide

choice in grades of printing papers. Even a poor negative may yield a reasonable print on the appropriate grade of paper.
The table given below summarises the faults in black-and-white negative processing which can be rectified as a last resort.

LAST-DITCH REMEDIES FOR PROCESSING FAULTS

Cause of fault	*After-treatment*
Under-exposure, correct development	Intensification
Under-development, correct exposure	Intensification
Gross under-exposure	Discard
Over-exposure, correct development	Reduction
Over-exposure and over-development	Reduction
Over-development, correct exposure	Reduction
Gross over-development or fogging	Discard

Colour processing does not allow for much margin of error and there are no procedures available for correcting mistakes if they do occur. Accordingly, the greatest possible care is essential in colour processing.

Glossary of Processing Terms

Accelerator – Alternative term for the alkali in developers (see page 64).

Acid – A chemical compound which contains one or more hydrogen atoms replaceable by a metal, e.g. *acetic acid,* to form a salt. Any solution with a pH value below 7 is acidic. Stop, bleach and fixing baths are normally acidic in nature.

Additive primaries – Red, green and blue colours, each comprising approximately one-third of the visible spectrum (see page 20).

Aerial oxidation – Oxidation of developing agents by air. Caused by excessive exposure of developers to the air and may give rise to fog and staining.

Agitation – Thorough movement of processing solutions during processing. Modern spiral developing tanks usually employ agitation by inversion (see page 67).

Alkali – A soluble chemical compound which combines with an acid to give a salt and water only. Any solution with a pH value greater than 7 is alkaline, e.g. sodium hydroxide, sodium carbonate, borax. Used as development accelerator.

Antifoggant – A chemical compound which, when added to a developer, inhibits fog formation, (see also *restrainer*)

Bleach – A processing solution which removes a silver image. Used in black-and-white reversal processing (see page 96) and in colour processing. In colour processing, bleaches convert the silver image to silver bromide which is then removed in a fixer (see page 89).

Bleach-fix (Blix) – A processing solution that removes both silver and silver halides from a colour film or paper.

Cartridge – A self-contained, easy-loading device containing, for example, 126 size film in which the film is wound from one light-tight chamber to another (see page 58).

Cassette – Light-tight metal or plastic container containing a light-trap through which the film leaves the container. Normally for 35 mm film (see page 55).

Clearing bath – A solution used in black-and-white reversal processing after the bleach to remove the bleach reaction products.

Colour coupler or former – A chemical compound which combines with oxidised colour developing agents to form a dye. Colour formers are normally incorporated in the emulsion (see page 87), but may be included in the developer (see page 132).

Complementary colours – Dye colours which are complementary to the additive primary colours red, green and blue, i.e. cyan, magenta and yellow (see page 22).

Contrast – The ratio of the light transmitted by the most transparent to that transmitted by the most opaque areas of a negative or transparency. In a negative the tones may proceed from black to white in a large number of steps or a small number of steps. The former is termed low contrast and the latter high contrast.

Density – Exposure followed by processing produces a 'blackening'. Quantitative measurements of blackening are densities.

Developer – A solution which converts the invisible latent image into visible metallic silver. The active ingredient is a developing agent or agents, in conjunction with a preservative, accelerator and restrainer (see page 64).

Emulsion – The name given to a light-sensitive dispersion of silver halides in gelatin which is coated on a support.

Fixer – A solution for removing silver halides from emulsions. In negative processing, fixing follows development and removes the unexposed silver halide grains. In colour processing, fixing removes the unexposed silver halide grains, together with silver bromide formed in the *bleach*. A typical fixing agent is hypo, or sodium thiosulphate pentahydrate.

Fog – A visible image or density in a negative not forming part of the image. May be caused by stray light or excessive development.

Gradation – Tone scale or contrast range of a developed image (see *contrast*).

Highlights – Brightest parts of the subject which are recorded as the darkest parts of a negative or the lightest parts of a positive.

Hypo – Popular name for sodium thiosulphate pentahydrate.

Integral tripack – Is the basis of modern colour photographic materials in which a red-sensitive layer, a green-sensitive layer and a blue-sensitive layer are coated on a film or paper base (see page 20).

Intensifier – A solution which is used to increase the density, with or without an increase in contrast, of a black-and-white negative.

Latent image – A photographic emulsion forms a latent or invisible image on exposure to light, which can then be made visible by a developer.

Latitude – The range of exposure over which a photographic film will give an acceptable image.

Mask – A means of correcting colour reproduction. The mask is usually used to correct for dye imperfections of the cyan and magenta dyes, and in a typical colour negative is orange in colour.

Monobath – A single processing solution which functions both as a developer and a fixer.

Negative – An image in which the opaque areas correspond to the brightest areas of the subject and the transparent areas correspond to the shadows of the original subject (see page 15). A colour negative has colour as well as tone recorded in the opposite sense to the original subject (see page 20).

One-shot processing – A method of processing in which the solutions are used once only and then discarded.

Positive – A transparency or print in which the opaque or dark areas correspond to the shadow areas of the subject and the transparent or light areas correspond to the brightest areas of the subject. A positive colour image will have image colours which correspond to the colours of the subject.

Preservative – A chemical (such as sodium sulphite) included in a developer to inhibit aerial oxidation of the developing agent and to prevent developer oxidation products from staining the image.

Printing – Process in which an image is made by exposing a sensitive material to light passing through a negative (or transparency). May be carried out by contact printing or enlarging (see page 16).

Reducer – A solution which is used to decrease the density of a silver image with or without a change in contrast. Photographic reducers are not reducing agents, but are oxidizing agents in chemical terms.

Reducing agent – A chemical compound which transfers electrons to the species being reduced, e.g. developing agents are reducing agents in that they transfer electrons to silver ions (Ag^+) to form metallic silver (Ag).

Restrainer – A chemical added to a developer to inhibit fog formation, e.g. potassium bromide.

Reticulation – Mosaic-like appearance of the film with a wrinkled surface. Caused by subjecting a film to a sudden temperature change during processing.

Shadows – Areas of the subject which are not illuminated and are represented on a negative by the least dense areas and on a positive by the most dense areas.

Silver halide – Term for compounds of silver with the halogens (fluorine, chlorine, bromine and iodine). Silver bromide, chloride and iodide form the basis of the light-sensitive constituent of photographic materials *(emulsions)*.

Stop bath – An intermediate bath used to stop development before further processing steps are carried out. They are acidic in nature (e.g. 1 per cent acetic acid).

Subtractive primaries – Alternative term for complementary colours.

INDEX